UNDERSTANDING BILLIARDS AND SNOOKER

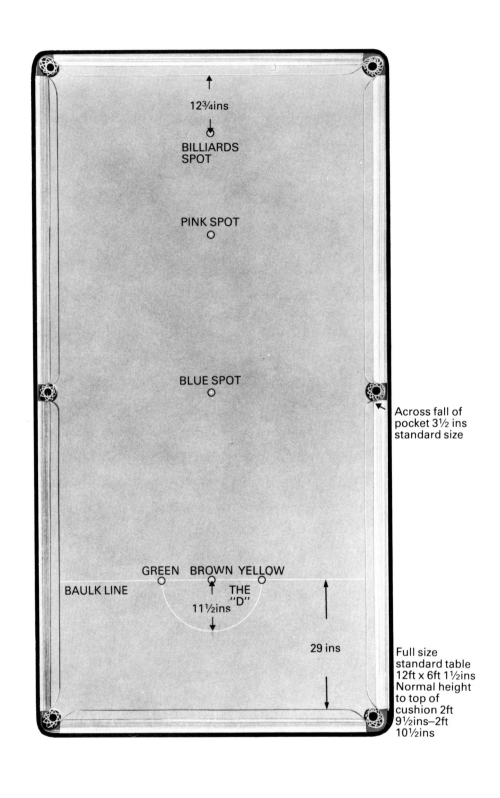

12¾ins

BILLIARDS
SPOT

PINK SPOT

BLUE SPOT

Across fall of
pocket 3½ ins
standard size

GREEN BROWN YELLOW

BAULK LINE

THE
"D"

11½ins

29 ins

Full size
standard table
12ft x 6ft 1½ins
Normal height
to top of
cushion 2ft
9½ins–2ft
10½ins

Pelham Pictorial Sports Instruction Series

Jack Karnehm

UNDERSTANDING BILLIARDS AND SNOOKER

As adopted by the Billiards and Snooker Foundation

Pelham Books

First published in Great Britain by
PELHAM BOOKS LTD
44 Bedford Square
London WC1B 3DU
1976
SECOND EDITION JUNE 1983
Reprinted 1984

ISBN 0 7207 1455 9

**Printed in Great Britain by
Blantyre Printing & Binding Co. Ltd**

Colour photographs by Peter Hurwood; black
and white photographs by Roger Blake and Tom
Finnane.

Contents

Part One   A New Approach To Understanding

Part Two   The Player—Technique

To All Players

Throughout my playing career I have tried to give back to the game something in return for all that it has given me, so that much of my time has been devoted to helping others to improve their play and to appreciate the skills involved.

During my days as Chairman of the B.A. & C.C. (as it was called), the National Coaching Scheme was founded.

Now as a professional player and coach I feel it would not be amiss to thank all those pupils and players who have helped in their own way to make this book possible. The text and photographs are based on the questions most frequently asked by all grades of players, and I hope that you will find they offer inspiration as well as practical help.

Part One
A NEW APPROACH TO UNDERSTANDING

A New Approach to Understanding

What is it that seems to make billiards and snooker harder to play than most ball games? The time needed from learning to becoming a very good player is, with few exceptions, so long. Years of experience may make a person wiser but not a significantly better player. I hope you will find new and stimulating ideas in the pages that follow—so that you can apply fresh thinking, or maybe a different mental approach to your game, and then greater understanding and improvement will come quicker, bringing all the added pleasures that success or mastery give, not to mention the wider benefits to the sport itself.

Many words have been written on billiards and snooker with a multitude of diagrams and illustrations and most of these works are very good indeed. However, during the last few years of my playing career I have given much time to individual and group coaching and I have found that most newcomers and many old hands at the game do not understand some of the finer requirements that are so necessary to help advance their play. One cannot blame them for this lack of understanding as many of the questions I have been asked have never been answered satisfactorily for them in print. The theory of the game is often presented in terms that can only be properly appreciated by players with natural flair and style.

The purpose of this book is to make you understand, perhaps for the first time, that the basis for all improvement in playing stems from good technique. This is the vital factor for any player wishing to make a steady advance in the game of his choice to whatever level he wishes to reach, even to the top if he feels so inclined to try his luck.

I cannot emphasise enough that unless a player has a technique that permits smooth and accurate cue action, whether by sheer natural ability or tremendous personal endeavour, he will never get to a very high standard of play. As a professional player and coach it would be very wrong of me to say otherwise. In my view, too much importance has traditionally been placed on diagrams showing the thousands and thousands of theoretical shots—in this book I will concentrate on the elements that make up sound technique and correct mental attitude to the game, and use only those photographs and illustrations that will make a practical contribution to your game.

Understanding Billiards and Snooker

Everything Depends on Technique

The basic techniques required to become a good player apply to players of any class. It is the effort and application of the individual that brings eventual success, to whatever lengths he is prepared to go and the ambitions he wants to fulfil.

However, it is not enough to have the determination to play every possible hour at your disposal unless you play or practise correctly.

A club player, content with his one evening a week, is quite happy to get his style somewhere near the mark and be content with the occasional 30 break, although I suspect that underneath there is always the desire to do better than the other chap.

The ambitious player will tighten up his technique until his breaks increase towards 50 and over ; his ability to master the cue, which means to apply stun, side, screw, and 'run through', pot consistently well, and judge the angles correctly, and his reading of the table will unfold further and further to spur him on to greater achievement.

This is so easy to say but very difficult to do. The difficulty comes from the very nature of the game ; it is played on a true surface where faults created must generally be the mistake of the player rather than the elements involved. So small is the margin for error that great care is needed and this creates tension. Unlike football, cricket, and pretty well all other ball games, there is no free movement either in stance or with balls in play. The only movement before the moment of truth is an accurately controlled arm action—so that tension,

piled upon self-pressure to perform well, creates physical and mental disharmony to an alarming degree. So right does the mental and physical co-ordination have to be that seemingly minute and unaccountable lapses in the 'count-down' to the shot are enough to make it a miss. The answer lies in correct technique in addressing and striking the cue ball. The game is an art and many of its severest tests of skill are called for *before a ball is struck*. This is a fundamental fact—to understand it is to be given a valuable key ; to acquire good technique is to open the door to all the pleasure and riches the game can offer.

The Good Player

Every time you pick up your cue to play you realise how difficult the game is, and yet when you see good players playing it seems so easy. What do you think is the basic reason for the difference, and how do you go about making yourself a first-class player ? It is not just a question of learning the rules and getting on the table and hitting the balls willy-nilly.

Let us start by looking at the good player, picking the points that appear to show through in his play. Let's say that the first impression is one of quietness, concentration, and smoothness in potting the balls ; the lack of force that is used and yet the balls seem to travel so easily and so far.

I think the point that is missed by the average player is that while a good player looks to be playing with a certain amount of ease and comfort within himself, he has in fact worked very hard at the game, and probably has a strong natural flair. His hard work has created a good technique—good timing and co-ordination of the muscles in co-operation with the eyes, which together produce a poetry of motion characterised by an air of nonchalance and ease. A club player will often try to model his style on a very good player which is commendable, and he will also try to imitate the ease in which the good player plays and in doing this he will often be unable to apply the real effort, concentration, and accuracy of striking demanded because the man who seems to be playing very easily is in reality playing very hard. He has got this down to such a fine art he is able to control himself and not allow this to show through to any great extent. It is only when the pressure builds up in extremely tense matches between two very good players that you can sometimes see one player or the other begin to break a little and his technique let him down, but this is at a much higher level than the average club player.

The Beginner

So what really has the beginner got to learn ? First and foremost that unless he acquires good technique he will never become a good player. The first essential is to seek expert advice in the form of coaching because it is most important from the beginning to develop a good technique and understand the game and what is required. The natural reaction of any learner, particularly the younger ones, is to hurry through the

A New Approach to Understanding

preliminaries and try to get results from playing. They tend to sacrifice technique just to get on a table and have fun. If you do things in the correct order, develop technique, and master cue action, you can perform various shots from which you will see control coming into your game. This control is very difficult to acquire by indiscriminately knocking the balls around, or when trying to play a serious game against another club player or friend. It is far better to become a master of, shall we say, 10 shots that can be performed consistently than to play every shot off the cuff and hope that you are going to do the right thing.

Always a Moderate Player

During a recent coaching session I was asked by the pupil concerned why it was that he consistently made his 30 and 40 breaks with a top break of 79 yet could get no further with his game, and it occurred to me that this situation could well apply to thousands of players around the country.

Going back further still I can remember when the average billiards player faced a similar situation. Having played quite well for a break of 40 or maybe 60 he would then fail when approaching his top break of 80 or so. So the problem exists for the snooker and billiards player alike—if I can play this well, why is it I cannot get further with my game ? It must be fair comment to say that the reason is either lack of knowledge or lack of the ability to apply the knowledge. Both topics in my opinion can be pursued by the player concerned to his

Understanding Billiards and Snooker

practical benefit and to his enjoyment and appreciation of the skills of the game when he is a spectator. Should he by chance be the spectator holding the other cue, the greater will be his appreciation of his own need to acquire superior skill!

Now I have consistently noticed when coaching players that, whether they are the '30-breakers' or promising high-class players, when they come to the shot so critical to the continuation of a nice size break, they fail because they do not apply just that right amount of cue ball control, although they knew or felt it was within their powers to do so. So what happens? So often have I been witness to this scene that I am sure the reasons that cause this to occur so consistently belong to a phase of the game not usually studied or understood and having nothing to do with ambition or experience, *it is the mental and physical approach to the shot*—a vital part of technique.

Understanding is the Key

Let me assure you that unless you do understand the importance of good technique there will not be enough hours in the day to help you bring your game up to the level you so earnestly desire.

At first the thinking out of your shots may seem a trifle irksome but like all things practice brings a measure of success and after a while the theory will fade to the back of your mind and allow you to perform in a co-ordinated way which will delight you, until such time

as you need to call on your knowledge to help you beat the other fellow.

Remember as you get better in your play, improvement becomes harder to find, and experienced players will go to any lengths if they believe that what they have in mind will improve their game.

Value of Coaching

Since writing my first book (*Billiards and Snooker,* Pelham Books, 1973) television and commercial sponsorships have given a tremendous boost to snooker. The popularity of the game has never been higher and is still growing. In consequence the thirst for knowledge has increased and I am quite convinced that this will eventually lead to higher standards of play at all levels including the professional game. Such has been the demand that much of my time has been taken up with advising and teaching at all levels of play. Having been a student of the game for a considerable number of years with a fair degree of success, the experience of these last few years has made me realise how the up-and-coming player searches and struggles for knowledge in his own way to improve his play in all its aspects—rarely achieving either genuine improvement or knowledge on which to build his game. Formerly only the fortunate few got to a good club standard and went on to real championship class, but with the popularity of the game now growing so fast, the opportunities will be available for players who are keen enough to make a name for themselves. The only basis on which this improvement can be achieved is with deeper understanding of the fundamental techniques.

The Karnehm Method of teaching is not confined to snooker: its aim is to teach the correct basic techniques for a player to gain maximum pleasure from his efforts on a billiard table. The method is based on perfection, not on how any one famous player plays. The top player at billiards, snooker or pool has never and will never reach perfection, simply because temperament, in whatever form you wish to describe it, has a breaking-point which creates loss of co-ordination of mind and muscle, in other words a moment of lost concentration.

These moments of lost concentration may have nothing to do with the ability of two particular players in a match. Often the clash of personalities causes an upset of form, i.e. the breaking-point of one player or the other is reached. It is the person who combines a sound technique with a natural ability to play who is most likely to succeed. If he also has a suitable temperament and enjoys the fight then he can go as far as his dedication desires—until an opponent who has similar ambitions confronts him and the clash of skills in all its varying forms takes place.

It is at this moment in a match, which I might add comes at all levels of play, when sound knowledge and technique add strength to a player's feelings. It is feelings we are talking about that govern the emotions which form character. The self-imposed discipline required by a good player becomes more important—and very often more

A New Approach to Understanding

difficult—as he climbs the ladder of success.

Your Own Approach to the Game

The general pattern of questions asked by ordinary players is basically the same, and variations, of course, are endless ; what applies to one person may not apply to another. Indeed some players have an insatiable desire for information of a nature which, while giving hours of pleasure in effort of execution and no doubt many hours of conversation generally, tends to confuse the mind and make the end product seemingly impossible. But then who is to decide how a certain individual takes his pleasure from the game ? I know many players who derive little pleasure unless they have won their game and see nobody's play but their own. Who is to say which is the best way ? Each man to his own. The important thing is to play the game to the best of your own ability. The game generally portrays the character of the individual anyway. As you learn to use the cue so the game will unfold to amaze you with its astounding possibilities, and intricate little shots of delicate touch become available to you. Suddenly you are aware of the tremendous value of side in all its complexities and you are hooked, and you now realise how hard it is to strike the cue ball in the middle.

In my first book I kept to basics and the reaction of side, screw, and stun linked to shots to create a sound cue action. Now I intend to expand this approach to ensure that you fully understand what is

15

happening when you play, and you understand the technique required to enable you to play well.

There are many factors which together make up Technique. They are covered in Part Two.

Coaching for You?

It might help you in your quest for improvement to know what to expect from a qualified coach. An Area Foundation coach, i.e. a player who has been passed as eligible to teach youngsters the basics of play, does not have to be a top player. The main requirement is, in fact, a desire to help young people, and needless to say he or she must be an enthusiast of either billiards or snooker. The fact that they are qualified is assurance that the coach has enough expertise to teach to the requirements as laid down by the Coaching Foundation, a body sponsored and encouraged mainly by the Billiards & Snooker Traders Association. The aim

is to ensure that young people can seek the same advice and guidance, based on a sound method, in whatever part of the country they reside.

Official Foundation coaches are trained at Lilleshall National Training Centre to teach the basics of play only. It should be realized that a coach in any sport, however well qualified, does not set out to make a champion—he only helps his pupil to develop his talent to his highest potential. The player can only become a champion through his own determination and dedication.

The acceptance of some coaching, at whatever stage of a player's career, can save months and possibly years of struggle to achieve reasonable improvement. Bad habits developed in a player's technique can be extremely hard to correct, hence the value of learning the right way in the early stages.

The Billiards and Snooker Control Council, the world governing body, uses the Karnehm Method in conjunction with the Coaching Foundation, throughout the United Kingdom.

Part Two
THE PLAYER—TECHNIQUE

The Cue and Its Functions

Most players in their early days will use a cue from the rack and pick the best of a well-worn collection. Usually it is only when improvement shows that a player may decide to buy his own cue. Bearing in mind that a well-made cue of sound timber, if looked after and kept in a case when not in use, will not only last a lifetime but will also become as vital to your game as your own right arm, you should invest in a cue of your own as early as possible. The selection of a cue is a very personal thing and if you do not feel experienced enough to make the correct choice you should obtain expert advice. The longer you use your own cue, the more attached you become to it —top players rarely change their cues, if at all.

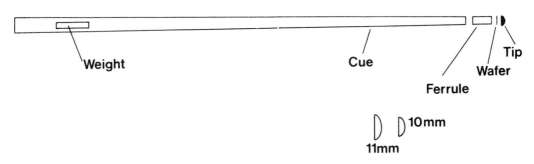

Figure 1. Cue/Ferrule/Tip

Normally cues are made in two types of wood, shafts being of maple or ash, and the butts of ebony. Other hard woods are often used but I personally think there is nothing to match the nice silky feeling of a well-polished ebony butt. Cue weights range from 16 oz. to $17\frac{1}{2}$ oz. approximately, but the weight can be varied by adding lead pellets to the butt at various distances to give the desired balance for each individual. Usually such balancing is done only to meet the special needs of an experienced player.

All cues should have a certain amount of whip in the shaft, enough to feel vibrations in the palm of the hand when

19

holding the butt, and striking the shaft against the other hand. Always try to ensure that the cue you use is straight ; rolling it on the table is a fairly good test but not always a true one. A perfectly good cue for playing purposes may not roll straight due to slight irregularities during manufacture as it comes off the lathe, but a line taken through the centre of the core of the cue will be straight as the Figure 2 shows.

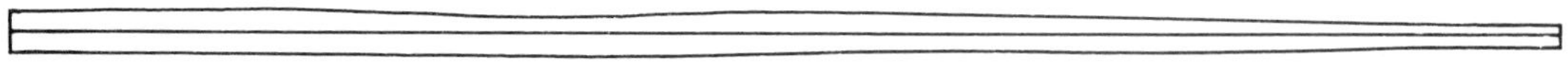

Figure 2. Cue—straight centre line

Care of the Cue

A good cue will need respect rather than regular attention during its life. On days when humidity makes it 'sweat' or feel damp, it can be wiped with a soft damp cloth, and then wiped dry. It is, however, most important that you never lean on your cue when playing or awaiting your turn, and you do not lean it against the wall. A cue left at an angle against a wall, even for a few minutes, can become bent and rendered virtually useless. Make sure that you put it in the case when not in use.

Another suggestion you may find helpful is to develop the habit of always holding your cue in the same position— try holding it so its straightest edge is in line with the eyes. This will enable you to sight more accurately through the line of the shot.

No matter how perfect your cue, if the tip is not right for you, then you will never be happy with it or your game. In the next section I have explained in some detail how to choose a suitable tip.

Selecting a Tip

It is fair comment to say that the better the player the more he thinks about the tip he uses. From a box of fifty it is quite possible to find only ten that will suit you. As far as possible you should avoid the trial and error approach of putting on and taking off tips, which has an unsettling effect on your game, and can be disastrous when you are facing games that may be vital to you. So what should you look for ?

A tip must be firm but not hard. It needs sufficient resilience to allow slight compression to take place on striking the cue ball, so enabling it to grip the ball's surface while still retaining its shape. If the body of the tip is too soft it will sag and stay that way. You will have *felt* very little from the shot. On the other hand a hard tip will tend to skid off and give you a feeling of being powerless to hold the cue ball in control.

I have found the best way to find the most suitable tip is to hold a new tip edgeways and gently push a thumb nail into the side to feel how tightly the fibres are compressed ; the tighter the harder, the looser the softer. A tip can be likened to a concertina, if you can get both thumbnails into the edge and gently push and pull you will see what I mean. I prefer just the slightest movement but what suits me may not be right for you. Choice of a tip is a personal thing—so be guided by what you *feel* in play.

Tipping a Cue

These days there are so many instant adhesives available that choice is really the only problem. In my experience I have found nothing better than the green gelatine wafers (softened in hot water) for sticking a tip on to the cue. Not only is it a safe glue but it adds a little body to the substance of the tip and very often when a well-worn tip is due for replacement a further few weeks may be added to its life by re-sticking with two wafers together. This hint can be very useful if a crucial game is imminent and you do not want to break in a new tip. When fixing your tip make sure not to squeeze out most of the wafer, merely place the tip on the softened wafer and give the tip a couple of sharp taps with a file or knife handle and then leave to harden for half an hour or so before use. You should not leave the wafer in the hot water more than 10 seconds as the dissolving process takes away its thickness.

You will find that Blue Diamond or Elkmaster tips will shape quite well and not spread or alter to any extent when used. It is also important to make sure when trimming or shaping the tip that you do not open the fibres but that the filing or rubbing strokes are always made from the tip in the direction of the butt.

The tip should be slightly shaped to a dome rather than left flat—this is important to permit more accurate striking of the cue ball. With a properly shaped tip you can select your spot and strike it much more accurately.

Remember I have told you of my choice. Tips can be responsible for the best part of your game. Your form depends on them. It is no good having a good cue and a poor tip. Pay constant attention to your tip ; all you need is a coarse file, just occasionally press the cut of the file into the tip with the slightest turn, taking care not to drag on the fibres too much but rather to loosen the surface and free any hard shine that is on it.

Get to know the tip that is right for you. Feel it adding strength to your cue ball control, and confidence to your game.

Cue Delivery on the Line of Aim

I think it is as well that you have a clear understanding of what is required in terms of cueing or aiming the cue and that this applies to *every* stroke you play. In 2 the object ball to be potted into the pocket gives a straight shot through the cue ball and object ball. The line drawn is the line of aim. Being straight this makes recognition of the shot quite easy. The difficult thing to do is to extend that line of aim back through your cue hold thus keeping your cue on line precisely as your tip strikes through the cue ball.

Keeping all of the cue on the line of aim is the basic need to ensure a winner for every shot you play with centre ball striking, regardless of whether the angle is slight or acute. The cue must be kept on the line of aim with the butt behind the tip and on the line of aim at the moment of impact. 3 shows clearly that the cue is not properly on the line of aim —and as a result the pot cannot be made.

It is virtually impossible to get any shot you attempt if the butt of your cue is off the line of aim, and the butt can be off the line for a reason you may find a little misleading. The chances are that you are probably looking in all the right places through the line of aim *but only from the cue ball onwards* and the result is that your cue will not point where you are looking ! Marginal inaccuracies will mean failure with almost every shot. We are now talking not of eighths of an inch or even sixteenths but nearer sixty-fourths or even less with the striking of the cue ball. This is why it is so important to sight along your cue from as far back as possible. Be aware of your cue shaft in the whole field of view that you have of your shot. This will help to keep the whole cue on the line of aim.

The line of aim for the straight shots can be instantly recognised and this in itself creates confidence. Not that this means the shot is necessarily easier than an angled pot as in 4 but there is an added hazard with the angled pots— your eyes may leave the line of aim during the shot and go to the pocket in anticipation of the result or because of anxiety for the desired result. When this happens the shot will certainly be missed because the cue comes off the line one way or the other before the moment of contact with the cue ball, and you have achieved off-centre striking quite unwittingly. The disastrous effects this can have are explained more fully in the following section. Added to this your head pops up—shall I go on ? . . . or do you recognise the symptoms in that last game you played ? It is so important to keep your head down, *leaving your cue on the line,* and to keep looking along the line through the object ball until these elements of technique are working for you and not against you.

It is these things that you see in the professional player that you admire, but, maybe, you do not appreciate that they are being strictly carried out. When you try to do this yourself you may feel you are almost acting the stroke and taking too long in deliberating, but this is not so. Persevere until the operation of cue delivery feels normal, then when you slip back and play a bad one you will realise why you missed so often before you embarked on this fresh approach to play.

It is this realisation of what went wrong, or if you like, the understanding of yourself, that is going to improve your play, and give you added pleasure through skill and success. The apparent ease with which the professional player seems to operate is borne of hard work in co-ordinating his mental, physical, and optical faculties into a smooth controlled rhythm of play. Achieve this and the game becomes much easier. So much of this accuracy depends on another element of technique—stance.

In every shot you play *all* of the cue should be on the line of aim in order to get the pot or the result you intend.

On the line of aim
In photograph 2 the cue is correctly on the line with centre ball striking.

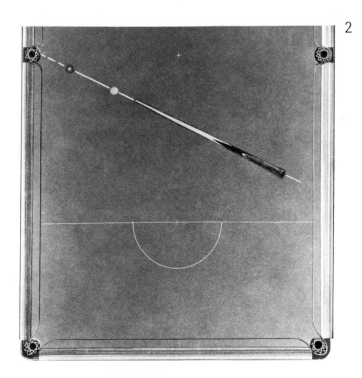

2

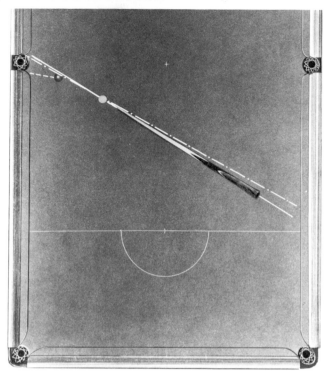

3

Off the line of aim

Photograph 3: When the butt of the cue comes off the line of aim as shown in 3 the pot will be missed. Here the broken line is the correct one for the shot being played and the single line is incorrect. With centre ball striking, the aim still appears to be correct from the cue ball onwards, but the error in alignment of the cue can be seen much more clearly from the butt end. This error should be corrected by repositioning the stance, starting with the feet.

The principle of aim applies to every stroke you play. The routine should be the same, pushing your cue through on the line of the shot and addressing the cue ball where you mean to strike it . . . that is the perfectionist way of playing.

Look through the object ball on the line of aim, strike through the line of aim, keep the cue on the line of aim, and do not let your eyes wander off this line and go to the pocket. This way you will find accuracy in your striking and in your delivery. If you anticipate the result of the shot your eyes will go to the pocket and this can happen before the tip of the cue actually reaches the cue ball. You will virtually be playing without looking at what you are doing and this is the prime cause for hundreds of missed shots especially the easiest ones. It is more difficult to keep your eyes on the line of aim when you play the more acute angled shots because of the added anxieties involved.

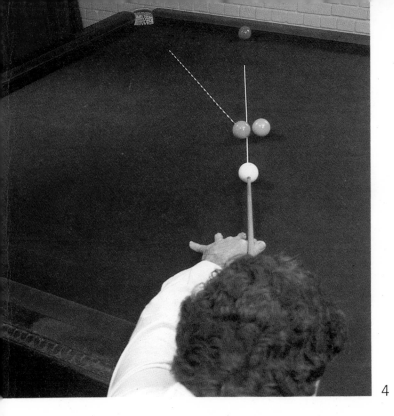

4

4 and 5 show the pink being potted off its spot, with a ball placed on the line of aim on the far cushion as an indication where the cue should be pointing. After the pink has been potted you will see that my cue is still on the line of aim pointing at the ball on the far cushion. Practise this finish to every shot you play.

5

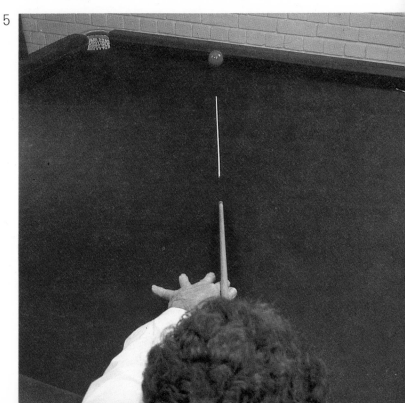

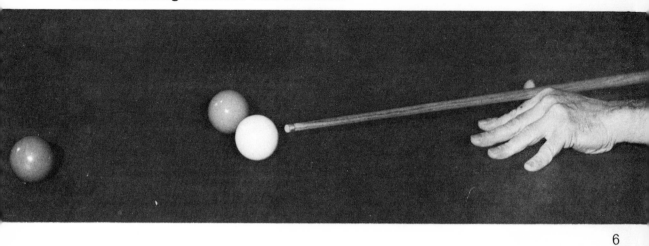

6

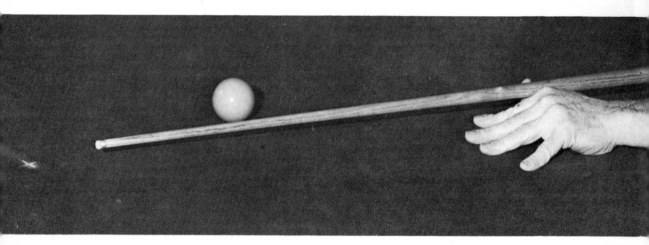

7

Follow-Through

These two 'before' and 'after' photographs show the position of the bridge hand and cue when addressing the cue ball. The amount of follow-through on the cue after the white had been struck was 7 in.

Stance

We have already seen that if all of the cue is not on the line of aim the shot will be missed. If the stance is faulty then it is almost impossible to put the cue on the line of aim. Why is this? Perhaps an optical term may help you to understand: 'Collimation'—adjusting a telescope so that the line of sight is in the correct position in relation to the mechanical axis of the telescope. If the light rays passing through a telescope are not properly aligned you will never see accurately with it. Similarly the relationship between stance and the line of aim— is a form of collimation—or we could say *we have to align the optical with the mechanical.*

Too often when a learner gets down on the shot he takes up what he thinks is the correct aiming position and prepares to strike. When told he is actually aiming 6 in. to the wrong side of the pocket he finds it hard to believe that what he thinks is right for him is really wrong in truth, so when told to correct his aim he has to aim what appears to be incorrect to him in order to score, which creates utter confusion, more so when he still misses. *He invariably thinks the correction but does not make it,* hence further confusion. This common mistake by beginners nearly always stems from faulty stance.

Get the Feet Right!

In my view the most important part of coaching is getting a pupil to develop a sound stance. When this is achieved so many of the other problems of cueing and aiming are minimised. So let us try to take stance and the approach to the table in its correct stages. I have found that most players adopt what they consider a stylish stance which has a built in position for comfort; then getting down to the shot they proceed to sway or move the trunk of the body to get a line on the shot. *It is this initially wrong approach to stance that creates so many of the problems for future play.* If you find yourself adjusting your body but not your feet you must be aware that your feet will not be set in the right place in relation to the line of aim and the shot is destined to fail. Watch a really good player and note how he steps into his stroke and seems to drop straight on to the line, just occasionally will you see a slight reshuffle of the feet to correct a misjudgement from the initial steps into the stroke.

Stance is something you can feel—by that I mean the placing of the feet, the slight twist of the body, and the pressures on the legs. At first twinges will be felt in various parts of the body

27

including the shoulders, which pupils have told me lead them to believe they were adopting an incorrect position. Hence the misguided view that comfort is essential when playing. Of course it is essential but only after you have learned to adopt the best position as an individual. Anything worth having is not come by so easily, if it were, all leading sportsmen would not have to train and practise so hard.

The Karnehm Method

Stance is governed by the position of the feet which means that those of us with long legs or short legs must compromise, and use some discretion with regard to placement, but there is no reason why a good stance should not be possible. The line of aim is the constant factor. The following method—the Karnehm method—will enable you to check for yourself the correct way to step into every shot. With the blue on its spot, place the cue ball midway between the blue and the near-centre pocket, in line with the opposite centre pocket. The line of aim is now clearly definable through the shot. In the photographs (8 to 13) I have continued the line right back through the stance. This extended line of aim is something that becomes clear and more definable the more you play and the more confident you become. Experience and confidence complement each other.

Place your right foot with your toe cap on the line and pointing to the centre of the end cushion rail, at the same time measuring your distance from the cue

ball. Place your left foot in a comfortable forward balanced position as indicated, pointing the toe towards the far middle pocket parallel to the line of aim. Without moving your feet stand up, with both legs straight, and you will find that you are facing the righthand far corner pocket. Point your cue at this pocket, the butt held to the centre of your stomach as in 10.

By twisting your body 45° bring the cue parallel to the line of aim but do not change the position of the feet. If you now get down to the shot (keeping your right leg straight, bending your left leg, and putting your weight forward) you will *feel* the bracing of the stance in the legs created by the 45° twist of the body. This is the correct feel you must have in your stance to avoid sloppiness. The left knee appears to press towards the right leg. Your left arm should be firmly thrust forward into a position that you feel is justified for the shot—either straight, or slightly crooked, whichever gives you the best support in your stance.

It is most important that, when approaching your shot to find the line of aim, you place your feet correctly in the standing position *before* getting down on the stroke. If you face the shot front-on with feet astride you will either be off the line when you get down or off balance allowing unwanted movement or sway to upset delivery of the stroke.

The Feel of the Stance

Once you have this appreciation of what is basically right, the feel of the stance is with you forever, and guided by your own judgement you will step into the correct stance on the line of aim for your future shots. The twist of the body will give your cue butt freedom of movement for proper cue action and follow through. The bracing of the shoulders as you prepare for the stroke will make your action feel smoother. Try if you can to sit on your back leg, the right in this case, to enable you to get low and look along the cue when sighting your shot. Cultivate the bend from the hips when getting down, giving you a straight back, rather than an arched one. This is very important in helping to get your cue down at the butt, so that it runs parallel to the bed of the table.

Make sure that you feel solid, and balanced slightly forward, in your stance. This is extremely important. Experiment until you are not over-reaching when striking the cue ball (or too close to it), and endeavour to govern this distance from the cue ball by the position of your feet, particularly your back foot.

When this method of bracing your body comes naturally to you, you will have a feeling of strength at the table instead of uncertainty, especially when pressure is on you from your opponent. The strength that a good stance can give you will add tremendous confidence to your play—a very great built-in asset.

9

10

Photograph 8 shows all that we are trying to achieve in stance so imprint it on your mind. You will note that I have taped a line through the centre of both middle pockets, extended that line down the side of the table and along the floor and this is the line of aim for the shot illustrated, which is to pot the blue into the opposite middle pocket.

Stance, as I have already explained, is the beginning and end of your playing technique. If you have a bad stance you will get so far in the game but no further. Stance has to be right if you want to make progress. In coaching I found that stance was the most difficult problem of all for the beginner and for the coach. I therefore developed this method which will give you a clear understanding of what you are trying to do so that you get a feel *for correct stance rather than trying to put yourself in the right place.*

When you are down on the shot you should feel good, strong, and well-balanced. This feeling of composure starts with the feet so look again at 8.

Take the first opportunity of trying out this method for yourself.

(1) The right foot is pointing to the centre of the end cushion of the table, and the instep is across the line. The left foot is placed at a comfortable distance in front of the right foot and to one side so that the left toe is pointing parallel to the line of aim in the direction of the shot (see photo 8).

(2) Without moving your feet stand up straight and you will find that you are facing the righthand corner pocket (photo 9).

(3) If you now put the butt of the cue to the centre of your stomach you will

10A

have to turn your body 45° to place your cue parallel to the line of aim for the stroke (photo 10). 10a is a side-view shot of 10 and clearly shows the amount of body turn, at no time moving the feet. Going halfway down to the shot (10b) shows how the body is braced even further as the left shoulder is turned towards the tape and the bridge hand placed on the tape, the body at no time leaning away from the vertical position.

10B

(4) *You will now feel the firmness on your body. While maintaining that twist, bend forward on your left knee, and place your hand on the line of aim. Keep your right leg stiff and you will find that as long as you have kept the twist on your body there will be tension on your left knee. The twist and strength of the stance are apparent from photo 11, which is a back view of 8. You are now ready for the shot, assuming your feet are correctly placed.*

33

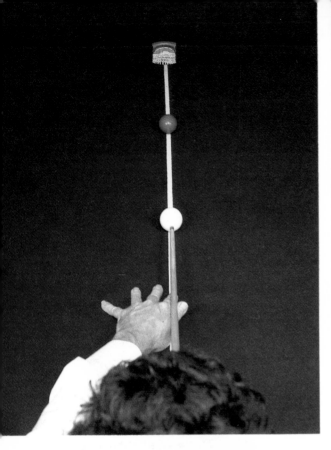

12

(5) *The bridge hand with the crook of the thumb and the forefinger precisely on the line of aim create the channel for your cue to address the cue ball in the centre. Provided you have placed your feet in the correct position in relation to the line of aim, your cue will be a continuation of that line. (Note how the tape in 12 and 13 is obscured by the cue which is running directly over it—that is dead on the line of aim.)*

I have found the Karnehm method works very well for all types of people irrespective of their height or length of arm, because it covers all elements of stance and gives a clear understanding of what is required. Of course there will be very slight variations in the distance between the feet and how far to one side the left foot is placed. (The principles of

13

this method apply equally to lefthanded people and there are no complications whatsoever.)

A little practice and perseverance with this method can save many hours of struggle and effort in trying to discover by trial and error what is correct.

14

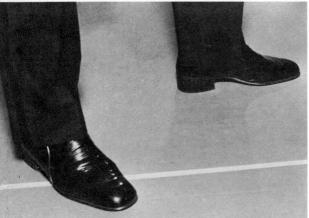

Stance—Feet Positions

14 Correct stance. Right foot on line of aim, left foot parallel to line of aim. Note the distance you feel that slightly exerts you when you twist to get down to the shot. Firm and solid.

15a Not quite good enough. Left foot not parallel.

15b Left foot too close to line of aim. Common fault. Loss of balance.

15c Both feet wrong. Too close together.

15d Both feet wrong, left foot especially. Very bad balance all round.

15a   15b   15c   15d

Stance—Forearm Positions

16 shows the well-stretched bridge arm extended to the full and all the weight and pressure is taken by the bridge hand alone as there is no part of the forearm on the bed of the table. Very often the shorter person can adopt this stance and find it quite satisfactory. The taller, or rangy person, very often benefits from having his forearm on the table as shown in 17. He can cuddle up to the stroke a little and get that crook in the arm rather than extending it really stiff and rigid and pushing himself too far away from the shot.

Resting the forearm on the table can also be suitable for shorter players. I am only 5 ft. 9 in. and have short arms, but find that on many occasions by resting my arm slightly on the table I get a feeling of added security and steadiness in my stance.

16

17

Cue Hold

The seemingly mysterious and fascinating effects obtained by a skilled professional stem from his hold on the cue. Rarely do spectators watch the hand that holds the cue, but rather the end that propels the cue-ball into action. Not that much would be seen anyway, so quick and slight are the squeezes and little flicks of the wrist that spin the ball on its way. So much do the fingers holding the butt, and the wrist, work in harmony to get the desired effects that I find it hard to separate them in describing their respective functions.

The hold must be soft but firm, working in conjunction with a supple wrist, if and when required. The correct cue hold is made by holding the butt softly with all the fingers, *keeping the little finger in constant slight pressure, gradually easing off on the remaining fingers so that the forefinger is merely a cradle.* This way you will find that your wrist will be a little more controlled in its back and forth motion for the various screw and side effect shots. There is a general tendency to hold the cue with the forefinger and thumb far too severely which cramps cue delivery, particularly the follow-through. The thumb merely acts as the door to the hand, closing it to keep the butt in position without any pressure.

The wrist needs to move forward with the forearm in delivery adding that extra thrust. This flick in the delivery can be varied with great control when mastered and the effects can be seen to advantage in slow screw and very deep-powered screw shots. To the experts, and the not so expert, these little movements are accepted and probably never thought about. However, to the not so lucky, and believe me there are plenty of them, explanation so often brings results much sooner.

Power From the Wrist

In order to play a really deep screw shot the cue hold must be momentarily transferred to the forefinger and thumb allowing the little finger and hand to open on the *last backward delivery* before striking. The hold returns to the back of the hand on the forward stroke, which then produces far more thrust from the wrist. The cue is virtually wedged into the back of the hand at the end of the stroke—*it is not suddenly gripped tightly* as this can create an early snatch effect and ruin the stroke. With this additional power combined with a smooth follow-through, the cue ball can really be made to fizz in a backward spin as it is propelled forward until it touches the object ball. It is when you get a full and accurate contact that your screw effect is greatest. Have you ever in your younger days, thrown a hoop forward with a flick of the wrist and tried to make it return to you? Well that is the sort of action required for screwing a ball.

The straighter you can keep your wrist in line with your forearm the better your chance of keeping a supple wrist with good control and accurate cue-ball striking. I know from experience many players seem to have to cock the wrist out of line and bad habits are hard to break. At all costs at least try to soften the hold otherwise your wrist will remain too tight and touch is lost to a very large degree.

In order to emphasise the need for a relaxed hold I have used the word 'hold' and not 'grip' throughout this section. Grip could mislead you into thinking that contact with the cue butt must at some point be tight. The billiard player is renowned for the general sweetness and softness of his play, indeed, the game demands it. While snooker may call for many screw, spin, and stun shots, these are not achieved any easier or better by adopting a different hold from that recommended.

Photographs 18–20 show the type of hold that I find most successful and that players generally seem to accept as normal. Control of the cue comes from the back of the hand, and pressures are usually firm but light.

It is this softness in the hold that helps the cue to follow through in its delivery.

A gentle hold keeps the wrist soft and flexible, and when you are following through it allows the wrist to give power to your hand. The shoulder is not pushed up on the forward thrust to cause any unwanted movement of the cue off line.

Much of the result of every shot depends on the feel and the touch contributed by the butt hand. Hold is a very important factor and should be well studied.

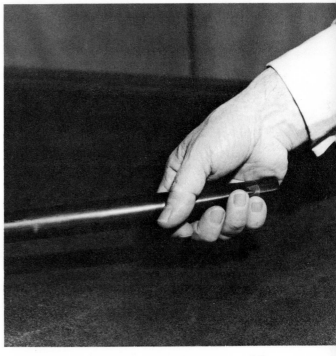

18

18 shows the cue butt hold in the normal position. Note the little finger is slightly pressing on the butt with the third finger showing slightly less pressure, the middle finger less still, and the forefinger acting as the cradle, with the thumb hanging loose merely to 'close the door'.

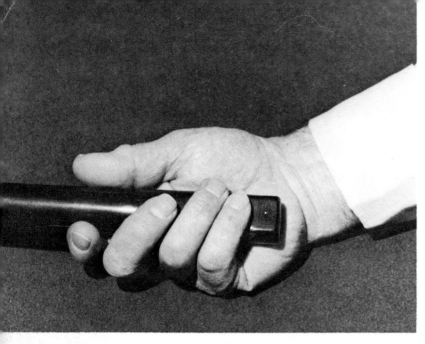

19

19 shows the hand turned over
without altering the hold in any way.
This gives a better view of the fingers, so
that you can see how the pressure eases
off to the front of the hand. I have taken
away the thumb from the side of the cue
merely to give a clear view of the fingers.

20 is a view of the other side of the
hand in the same position and shows
how soft the pressure is when the cue is
held normally. (Here the thumb is
tucked out of the way so that you can
gauge the pressure of the fingers on the
butt.)

20

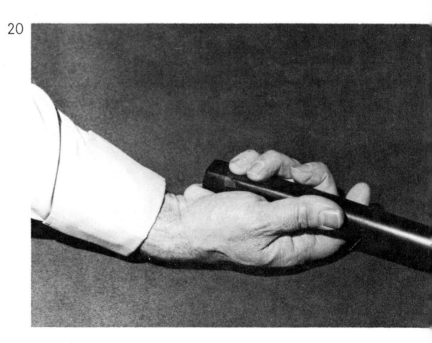

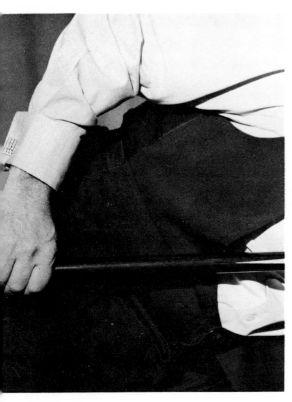

21a

Cue Hold—Power Shot

The power that the wrist contributes in screw and forcing strokes can be seen in this series of photographs. Note the position of the cue, which at all times is parallel to the bed of the table; the significant difference in the line of the knuckles, showing the pendulum movement of the hand on the cue; and the flick of the wrist that is employed. It is the opening of the hand on the backward movement that permits full power to the flick of the wrist as you go through on the delivery to the forward position. Note also the alignment of the hand, wrist, and forearm (all in a straight line), for all positions of the stroke.

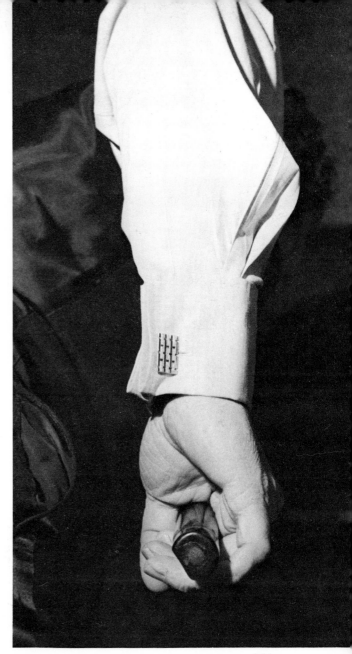

21b

(1) The backward position. *The back of the hand opens transferring the hold momentarily to the thumb and forefinger. The hold is a relaxed one, with no sign of tension—the cue is nicely cradled in the fingers. The forefinger shows a little, confirming that it is cradling not gripping the cue.*

39

22a

(2) Halfway through. *There is no tension in the hold on the cue, which is now transferring to the back of the hand. The cue is still doing the work. The thumb is hanging relaxed and is not exerting any pressure on the cue. Note here the line of the knuckles compared to the backward position.*

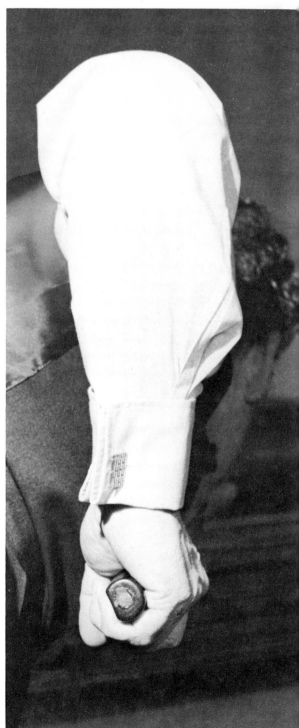

22b

23a

(*3*) Stroke completed. *The hold on the cue is still relaxed—it is not tensed. The forefinger can be seen sticking out slightly, proving the softness of the hold. Notice the shoulder has allowed the arm to drop a little permitting more forward thrust of the forearm.*

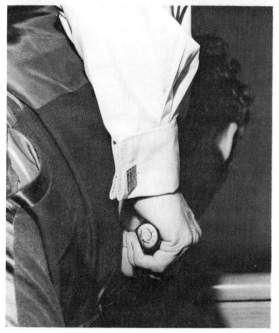

23b

24

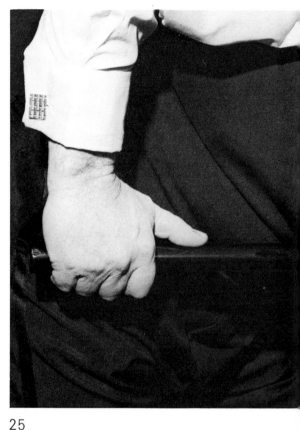

25

Hold—What Not To Do

24 shows many things that are wrong, and they are very common faults indeed. I know many good players that play like this but it certainly limits their possibilities. The cocked wrist, the elbow pulled in, the body a bit off line, are faults that players with ambition must correct.

25 shows exactly what not to do *with the butt hand and yet it is surprising how many players do this. If they do not have their thumb on the top of the cue they have it on the side. It can never be right. The wrist is tight, there is no freedom in the action whatsoever; it is not the way to play. The thumb should hang free and lightly close the door of the hand.*

Bridges

The bridge hand however it is made must be firm and unmoving until the shot is completed. The way a player puts his hand on the table is very revealing to an expert eye. One might liken it to a hand-shake when socialising. So often one sees the nervous uncertain player with a soft fidgety bridge hand and a vice-like grip on the butt. Precisely the reverse is necessary for smooth relaxed play. Much to my surprise, bridge hands seem to create many problems for players so that I feel it is worth showing them in some detail. It is the business end of the cue and plays as important a part as the other components in keeping the cue on line besides adding stability to the whole body. The following photographs will convey more than words, so I will only comment briefly on the different bridges shown :

(1) *The normal bridge hand.* The fingers should be evenly spread and the thumb should be well cocked to make a secure groove for the cue. It is important to keep the thumb fairly tight to the forefinger for smooth running especially for players with moist skin. A little experimenting will soon tell you just where to hold your thumb to ensure this.

(2) *The low bridge.* Merely turn the hand over, lowering the forefinger, raising the little finger and applying pressure to it to keep the hand firm and strong. You will need a low bridge for shots requiring well below centre striking of the cue ball.

(3) *The looped bridge.* This can be very useful when playing forcing shots or on many occasions when you feel your cue may escape in a tricky position. I find this especially useful when the cue ball is in that awkward spot off the cushion where there is not enough room for the hand to be placed. Always make sure your fingers are well braced with these bridges.

(4) *For playing alongside a cushion.* The recommended bridge is extremely satisfactory when used correctly. Do not be satisfied with something that looks like it but does not do the job. Remember, like stance, these factors are important and must not be skipped over as not so important.

(5) The most difficult cueing position, if that phrase need apply, is when *tucked up tightly on the cushion.* When this happens it is best to shorten your butt hold, slightly restrict your back-swing, and endeavour not to raise your head or move on the stroke. This of course applies all the time but in this particular case you may find that all these things seem to be

Understanding Billiards and Snooker

more difficult to control and this is caused by anxiety to perform the stroke with so little of the ball to strike. If power, or a fairly strong shot is needed, raise the butt slightly, brace your fingers on the cushion rail, and play as smoothly as possible.

(6) *When playing over the balls* pay attention to your feet for balance, as you are not only generally stretched in body but also your fingers will be on their toes, if you see what I mean !

Badly positioned feet cause body movement in this stroke resulting in the cue ball being struck in the wrong place —and the shot will be missed. Place your left or forward foot a little wider than for normal shots so that the leg will have the strength to resist the push of the opposite shoulder which rises as does the cue butt for this type of shot.

The Normal Bridge

26–29 show different views of the same bridge. The essential points are shown in detail because they are so important.

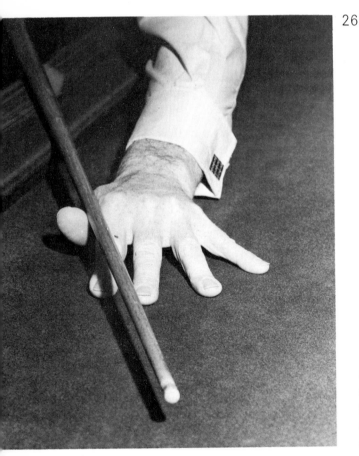

In 26 you will see the palm of the hand nicely placed on the table, the clear knuckles showing the pressure of the finger pads on the cloth, and a well-cocked thumb. Note that the wrist is also bearing on the table.

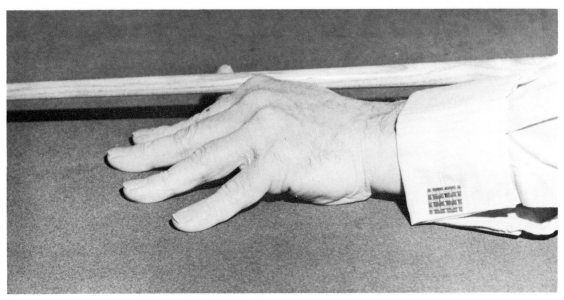

27

In 27 the palm is shown pressed into the cloth, and you can see the firmness in the fingers which are nicely spread. Note here that the fingers tend to arch not by bending but by pressure against the joints.

28 shows the top of the thumb, which is pressed well against the forefinger enabling the cue to run on the firmer part of the flesh rather than on an open thumb where the skin may drag on the cue, particularly in moist conditions.

28

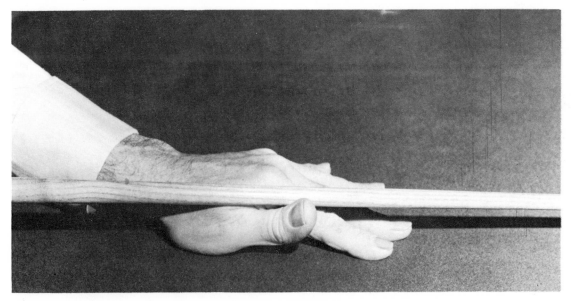

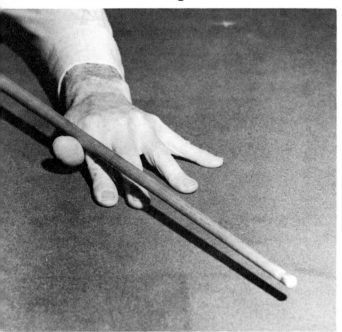

29

29 makes this even clearer. I think it is a point worth noting because it is often a problem for the beginner.

The Bridge for Screw, Deep Screw, and Side Plus Screw

30–32 show the type of bridge needed for screw, deep-screw, and heavy side shots combined with screw. Note that the hand is turned over, more pressure being put on to the thumb and forefinger.

In 30 you will see the knuckle of the little finger is showing the pressure that puts firmness into this bridge hand.

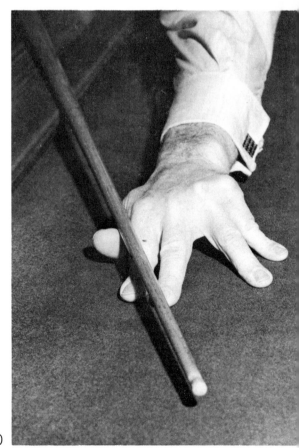

30

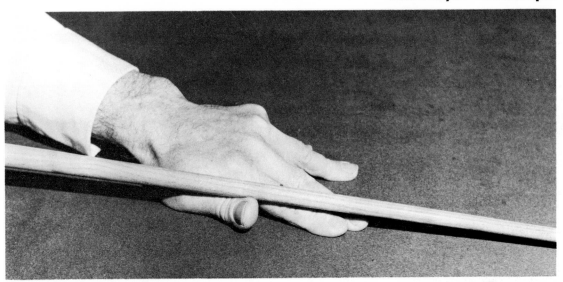

31

31, taken from the righthand side, shows the thumb being pressed well down on to the bed of the table but still tight to the forefinger. Note the tension applied by the little finger—again you can see the knuckle of the little finger standing out. A good bridge this.

32, from the lefthand side, shows the little finger pulled into the hand to apply pressure. Note the knuckle and the slight raising of this side of the palm of the hand in order to press the palm on the thumb side on to the bed of the table.

32

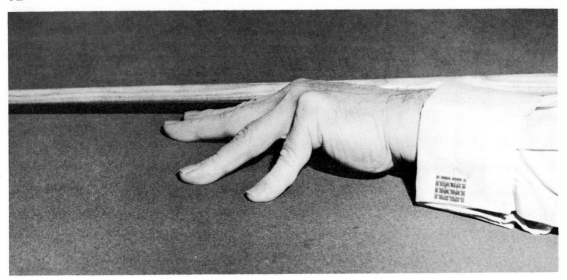

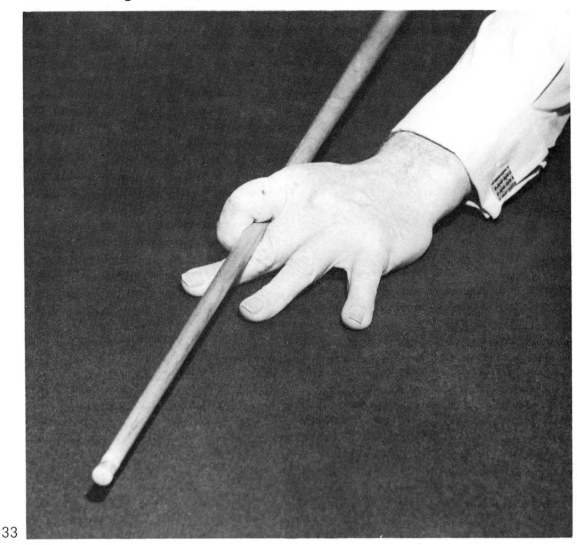

33

The Looped Bridge

I believe that the looped bridge is not used enough in the game. It is a very sound bridge that does not allow the cue to wander off line particularly in strong forcing shots, and at those times when your bridge hand is in such an awkward position that the cue can escape from the groove of the thumb and forefinger.

33 shows the hand flat on the table, fingers well extended, and the forefinger holding the cue quite firmly so that you have to push the cue backwards and forwards through the loop and can feel the friction.

48

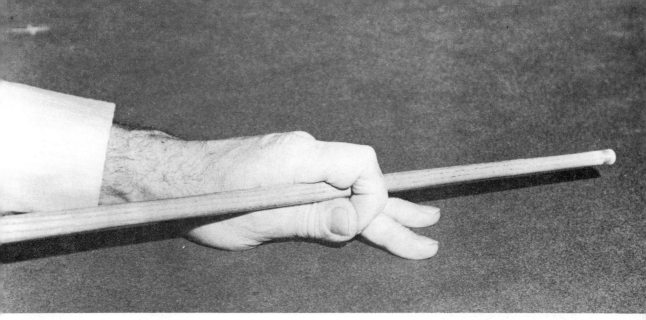

34

34 shows the righthand view of this bridge. The forefinger is looped and pressed well against the thumb to make a strong hold. People with long fingers often find they can complete the loop with their forefinger, but my fingers are too short to do this.

35 shows a looped bridge that is very useful when the cue ball is in that awkward position from the cushion where you cannot quite get your bridge hand on to the bed of the table, and if you keep your hand on top of the cushion you have too much overhang of cue before you touch the cue ball. Note the fingers pressed into the cloth and the comfortable support that the rail gives to the wrist.

35

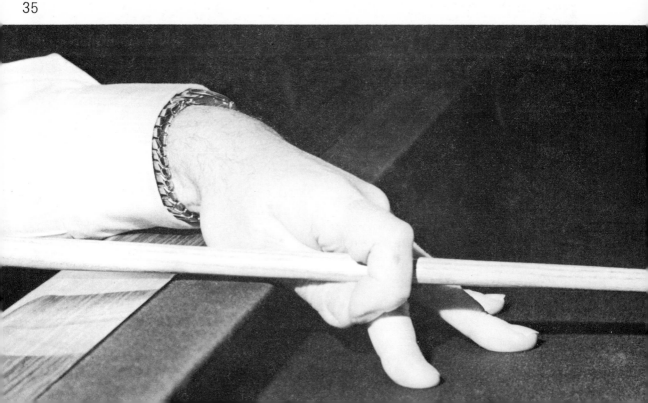

36

Cushion Rail Bridges (1)

37

Cushion rail shots always make problems particularly for beginners, who have extreme difficulty in getting hold of the cue in a comfortable and steady position. The different bridges shown in this section are the right ones for each situation and you will find they will strengthen your whole approach to difficult shots.

36 and 37 show the bridge to be used when you cannot make a normal bridge on the table. (If the cue ball is just a little further away from the cushion then it is necessary to use the looped bridge already illustrated.) In the bridge shown here the cue runs between the forefinger and middle finger with the thumb pressed against the edge of the cue for smooth running.

50

38

38 shows a familiar situation with the cue ball a few inches from the side cushion. For a good solid bridge the wrist is dropped to give a clear view of the shot. The forefinger is slightly bent to provide support for the cue running against the thumb, which in turn applies slight pressure to keep the cue on line and not allow it to wander. This of course is one of the main problems when you are tucked up on the cushion.

39 shows the cue ball very close to the cushion, here a little more power is usually necessary. To get purchase on the shot you should put your fingers on their toes as it were, and use your finger tips to get more power into the stroke. Note the firm pressure on the fingers indicated by the shiny knuckles, and the well-cocked thumb making a nice groove with the knuckle of the forefinger.

39

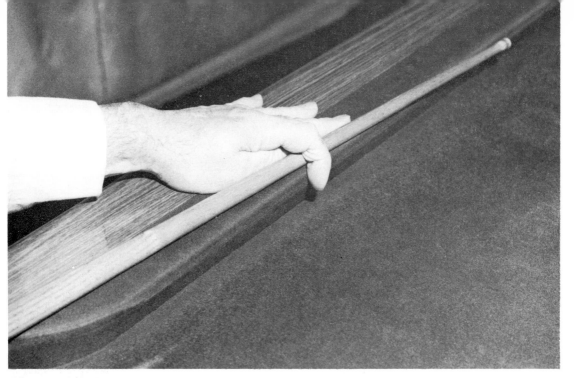

40

Cushion Rail Bridges (2)

40 shows an extremely useful bridge, which is sound and strong. In this bridge the cue runs against the thumbnail, which is tucked in beside the middle finger. The forefinger drops down the side of the cue and applies pressure against the cue which is also running along the pad of the middle finger.

In 41 you see the forefinger raised, showing how the cue is running along the thumbnail and the pad of the middle finger.

41

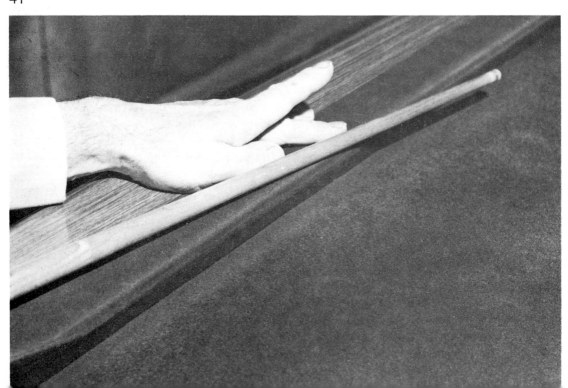

42 shows the front view of this bridge. You can see the thumbnail contact with the cue. Note how firmly the cue is held by the forefinger, with the pad of the middle finger pressing against the cue.

I cannot emphasise too strongly the usefulness of this type of bridge. There are so many slight variations depending on the angle of the cue as it runs along the cushion. Once you have mastered the bridges shown here they will unfold a hundred variations.

42

43

43 shows a good example of what I mean. Here we have the cue which has to be held almost parallel to the face of the cushion. This can be extremely difficult but by improvisation and applying pressure with the little finger along the cushion rail, the other fingers can drop on to the bed of the table and the forefinger can be hooked around the cue. You can see that virtually the same bridge is made to give good strong support to the cue.

44 again shows the cue a little further away from the face of the cushion than in 43, so the loop is rather difficult to make because you cannot quite reach the cue without having a very wide spread of the hand. Therefore instead of making the loop you place your fingers further into the table getting support off two fingers on the cushion rail and making a cocked thumb. You then have what is virtually a normal bridge, half on the cushion rail and half on the bed of the table.

44

45

Two Difficult Playing Positions

Photograph 45 shows one of the most awkward positions—playing over a cluster of balls when you have to come up to maximum height on your finger-tips. The shorter forefinger cannot reach the cloth so you tuck it out of the way, at the same time making a well-cocked thumb to give you a good deep groove for the cue to run in. Note the pressure of the finger-tips on the cloth for overall firmness of bridging.

56

46

46 shows a good action shot playing over a ball which is an inch or two away from the cue ball. In this bridge all the fingers can be placed on the table. This helps to keep the angle of the cue nearer to parallel with the table and gives a much firmer bridge hand. Again note the well-cocked thumb, pads of the fingers pressed into the cloth, and shiny knuckles—signs of a good solid bridge.

47

Using the Rest

The main point I want to illustrate when using the rest is that you must not let your elbow drop and bring your shoulder into the stroke.

By holding the cue with the thumb and forefinger, rather than with the whole of the hand as many beginners do, you get more flow into the stroke and it becomes a much more delicate operation than a thrust from the shoulder, which is the surest way to miss. Using the rest is the one time when everybody can do the

right thing in sighting, that is to look right down the cue from as far back as possible. Use of the rest makes this much easier to do. This is ideally how sighting should be done when you play normal strokes.

47 shows that I have tended to exaggerate slightly the height of my right elbow and by doing this it puts a little more pressure on the shoulder and gives extra freedom to the elbow movement.

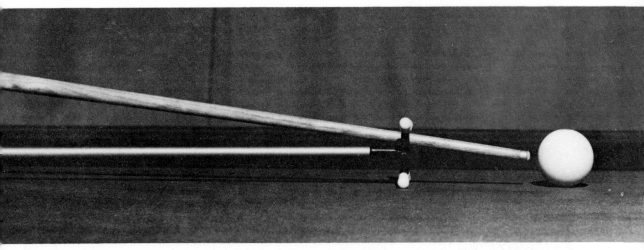

48a

Many players do not seem to be aware
of the special construction of the rest.
48a and 48b illustrate clearly the different
cue ball address when using the rest on
the shallow 'V' (48a) and the high 'V' (48b).
Note that the angle of the cue is exactly
the same in both cases. The shallow 'V'
gives centre cue ball striking and the high

'V' gives above-centre cue ball striking.
It is only when you need to raise the tip
of the cue for above-centre striking that
you use the higher 'V'—normally the
correct way to use the rest is with the
shallow 'V'. In the average stroke the rest
head should be about 8 in. from the cue
ball.

48b

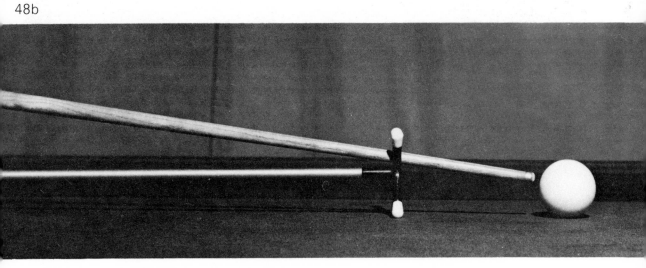

Centre Cue Ball Striking on the Vertical Line

'What happened there?' A remark so often made after a bad miss. Let me tell you. Ten to one you lined up for the shot with all the usual determination feeling you had it in the bag and, Whoops! another penny in the swear box. Somewhere in the countdown to the final delivery you go wrong, something flutters and however slightly the cue comes off line the object ball does likewise. You have not hit the cue ball where you meant to—it's as simple as that. Add to this any loss of rhythm or flow, maybe your head coming up, and you begin to realise that the cause of the miss lies in one or more faults in technique and not because anyone moved the pockets!

Address the cue ball where you mean to strike it. This gives your preamble to the stroke, or your preliminary strokes, a chance to impress your mind a little more to do precisely that thing. In doing this you are encouraging yourself to look along the cue and take the line of aim right through the shot, probably a little more than you normally might. All players, particularly newcomers, should concentrate on striking the cue ball up and down the vertical line. You would be amazed at the variations of control that can be achieved for positional purposes from maximum top to maximum bottom.

An Exercise in Centre Cue Ball Striking

Pot the black on its spot, the cue ball 18 in. away, for an angled pot into the corner pocket and see for yourself how top or bottom centre striking affects position. Now you will realise how wrist action in screwing, following-through, and stun has to be applied to get a thousand different results. The more mastery of the cue, the more shots in your locker. From the position I have described, try and make a break of 10 consecutive pots off the black spot without using left and righthand side, striking only *up and down the vertical line* to get position for another pot black into either corner pocket.

The effects of off-centre striking (on the horizontal line) are described in the next section—and because the cue ball will often be pushed off its true path, compensating factors have to be employed when aiming. To strike the cue ball off-centre, when you believed you were hitting it centrally, will mean that your line of aim (without compensations) will no longer be correct and the shot will be missed. It may be hard to believe but it is very difficult to strike the cue ball centrally—that is with absolutely no bias or side.

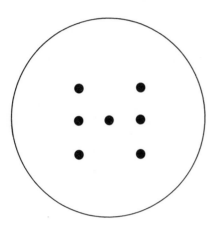 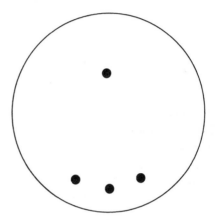

Figure 3. Points of cue ball striking

Full, $\frac{3}{4}$, $\frac{1}{2}$ and $\frac{1}{4}$-Ball Aims

Photo 49 (over) shows to advantage a simple way to explain and appreciate what is meant by these various aims. Using the snooker set as cue balls for demonstration only, the four shots, i.e. quarter-ball, half-ball, threequarter-ball and full ball, are on into the four middle and top corner pockets. The white object ball is on the pyramid spot. The pink is a full aim into the corner pocket. The blue is a threequarter-ball aim into the same pocket. The yellow is a half-ball aim into the same pocket. The green is a quarter-ball aim into the same pocket and from the opposite side of the object white, also a quarter-ball into the middle pocket.

Pursuing this principle further, by simulating these positions around the other top end cushions, it can be seen how by this method you may familiarise yourself with a variety of shots. It is easier to make mental notes when you can see all the lines of aim drawn in as on the diagram. For practice purposes move the cue ball in on the line of aim from the cushion until you can form a good bridge hand to play the shots, then move back towards the cushions as you progress. This method will imprint on your mind the majority of angled pots required, and will test your technique to the full.

I think perhaps I should emphasise, in showing these half-ball, quarter-ball and

49

threequarter-ball shots, that the aim
must be taken with the cue on the line
of the shot, aiming the tip of the cue at
a particular part of the object ball. That
is to say that when playing your half-
ball, you must aim through the centre of
the cue ball to the edge of the object
ball. Of course, with a quarter-ball aim
you will find that you have to aim the
tip of your cue off the edge of the
object ball. This, of course, does make
the shot a little chancy, to say the least,
bearing in mind the accuracy required in
contact, but the individual will gradually
get accustomed to his own sighting and
recognise what he must do to pull off a
given shot.

The threequarter-ball aim is made by

aiming your cue through the centre of
the cue ball at the quarter section of the
object ball, àppropriate to the direction
in which you wish to send it. Once you
begin to find the correct aim to get a
given pot, practise it again and again to
imprint it on your memory. But never be
discouraged on the occasions you miss
a pot that you thought you had
mastered; remember that guarantee of
certain contact is quite impossible—and
this is what makes the game so
attractive.

It is not until you really get down to
potting that you begin to appreciate the
accuracy that is needed and just what a
tiny part of the ball has to be struck to
get the desired effect, and it is for this

reason that nowhere in this book will you find me referring to a contact. You will note that all the time we are taking points of aim on the line of the stroke and not on points of contact. In fact, if you are taking just an ordinary half-ball aim, your point of contact is different. Therefore, to refer to a half-ball or quarter-ball aim and also to a quarter-ball contact or half-ball contact would only confuse the issue and would have a detrimental effect on one's play.

After persistent practice at these fixed-position shots, you should find that, as you develop some mastery of them, the inbetween positions will not appear difficult; you will fall into line with them almost straight away. This set-position potting routine can be practised in other parts of the table. Practise the quarter-ball aim particularly; this is not quite so easily stored in your shots-memory as the half-ball, but with much practice you should be able to get it as consistently as the half-ball.

The sequence of shots I shall now describe could be used as a practice routine for any enthusiast or indeed a set piece which Foundation Coaches might well employ in their coaching school for the pupils, according to the standards of the individuals concerned. In this respect much depends on the judgment of the coach in his assessment of his pupils' capabilities as to how he applies his knowledge to them.

Having established our thoughts on stance and technique, it is now time to try it out and discover faults and correct them.

Centre ball striking of the cue ball has to be established with the delivery of the cue on the line of aim. The procedure of play I adopt in sequence A is as follows. Remove all the balls except the two on the top cushion. All the ball positions are 6 cm (2$\frac{1}{2}$ ins) apart. With the cue ball on the brown spot, play up the table between the two reds returning to baulk at a pace of at least two table lengths. When this is achieved with regularity add the next pair of reds by the black spot and try to

50

repeat the shot you have been playing, coming back through both pairs. As progress is made, continue to add further pairs of reds until you are faced with the shot in the photograph. As balls are added more pressure is felt yet the shot is the same. Patience and discipline are needed as balls become disturbed, which they surely will be. This routine will really make you try.

Understanding Billiards and Snooker

Screw Shot

Screwing a ball to some comes naturally but to most it is a mystery. To screw with expert control is always demanding and requires a lot of expertise. The first thing most youngsters want to do is screw the cue ball like a professional when of course the technique can only be developed as progress is made.

Feel is the word needed to describe screw shots, i.e. deep screw, soft screw etc. Nobody can tell another how to feel, it is a personal quality allied to timing and must be developed by the individual. Once he has recognised the feeling and aim he puts into the shot to achieve the desired result, he is well on the way to success. Practice will establish his skill to the extent of his ability. Remember also that too much thinking on the shot can destroy the desired effect, thus lowering confidence.

The best way to tackle screw and its effects is to play a shot routine that permits gradual progress—how gradual will depend on the individual. The following shot sequence will teach you how to apply side, screw and, above all how to feel. Start at the position indicated in the photo and play it until you get the cue ball into the corner pocket fairly consistently, using low striking and a touch of right hand side. Proceed to the next shot and discover the extra effort and control needed to achieve the same result. Continue round the semi-circle of shots and when they

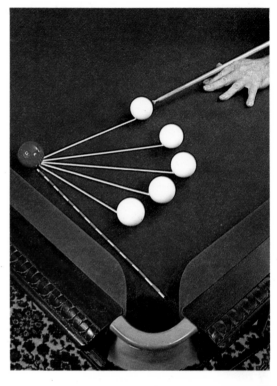

51

are within your power you will have no problem with screw shots. The accuracy with which you play them is dependent on yourself. The order of play, i.e. A, B, C, D, E, is important.

Points to watch for:
A firm yet soft hold on the butt.
Address the cue ball where you mean to strike it.
Leave your cue on line at the end of its forward final thrust.
Do not snatch at the delivery.
Keep your eyes on the object ball.

Off-centre Striking

You will no doubt have found in the pot black exercise in the last section that the use of side for positional purposes would help enormously but the pot becomes so risky that you play safety first just to get the pot. This state of mind comes to most players but if you are not prepared to overcome this problem then your game to a very large extent is going to stand still, and you will have joined the band of players who are sometimes good for a 30 but rarely make a 50.

The effects of off-centre striking are that the cue ball is initially pushed off the line of aim before pulling back in arc-like fashion. If you strike to the left of centre, the cue ball is initially pushed to the right, and if you strike to the right of centre it is initially pushed off to the left. While other factors can be involved let us for the moment deal with this basic fact. The greater the amount of side applied, so will the push-away of the cue ball be increased.

If all shots played with side (off-centre striking but on the centre horizontal line) are played at the correct pace for the table, the cue ball will pull back on to line before striking the object ball, but it will make contact *at a different angle* to that had it travelled in a straight line. (See photographs 52a and 52b.) Some compensation in aim is therefore necessary. So instead of being concerned about the push-off of the cue ball, alter the aim of the shot to the left or right of the centre of the pocket concerned.

An Exercise with Side

Let me give you an actual example, reverting to our pot black exercise. When potting the black into the righthand pocket with lefthand side centre striking, aim at the *nearside fall* of the pocket and you will find that provided you have imparted the side to your cue ball, the black will enter the centre of the pocket and your cue ball will check off the top cushion helping to make the angle for your return pot and keeping you closer to the black in the process.

From this one shot a whole series of shots can be discovered ; the use of strength, the amount of side permitting an almost unlimited number of contacts. The quality or smoothness of cue action will also show its effects in widening or narrowing the angles taken both by the cue ball and the object ball. Now perhaps you will begin to realise the importance of good cueing and cue ball striking.

Understanding Billiards and Snooker

Side and 'Throw'

Although side is not transferred to the object ball, it is a fact that the 'throw' of the object ball after contact with the cue ball struck with side (i.e. spin) will be different from the 'throw' effect created by plain ball striking. To see these effects for yourself place the pink on its spot with the cue ball 2 ft. away in line with the top corner pocket. *Aim at the centre of the pocket*, play with maximum lefthand side, and see the result. Mark the position *on the cushion* struck by the pink (for that is where the pink will go). Now reverse the procedure with a straight shot by *aiming at that same spot on the cushion* with the maximum opposite side on the cue ball, and Hey Presto ! you pot the pink ! Learn to recognise the amount of 'throw' you as an individual can impart to the object ball in this way.

Individual Ability

In my view no hard and fast rules can be laid down for the use of side in billiards and snooker. Assuming that we have match conditions any shots played at ordinary pace with not too much distance between the cue ball and the object ball can be predictably forecast by the expert. It must also be understood that the result expected or played for also depends on the quality of the cue action, timing, smoothness, and follow-through. The more expert you become with quality of cue delivery, the greater range of shots will be at your command. At times it is possible for the real expert to perform seemingly impossible shots through his knowledge of 'throwing' the object ball with side and making various compensations in aiming. I can personally play shots that seem to defy the normal 'rules' laid down for off-centre striking in the general run of play. The average player has little or no chance of performing these types of shot because he lacks the cue power needed to impart tremendous side effects to the cue ball with considerable accuracy, and he does not have the necessary discipline of technique.

Individual Rules

The only reliable rules anyone can follow on side and its use, are those made by himself for himself. They will change as his ability improves. It is only when a player begins to understand the precision of cueing and timing required that he treats side with the respect it deserves and so improves his play.

As your proficiency with the use of side increases so your repertoire of shots will increase and your next shot will be easier than it used to be. This does not intend to suggest in any way that a player must keep looking for the opportunity to play this way but merely to employ side with skill when required to continue on an otherwise free-striking break, or to put it another way, when you get to the 30 break area.

Do We Not Know It All Yet?

Perhaps no one can say what the ultimate possibilities with side are.

Future feats of ball-bending technique may yet make us gasp in disbelief, or wonder how it was we never thought of it ourselves. Side is such a complex subject that perhaps we have not yet seen nor appreciated its full potential.

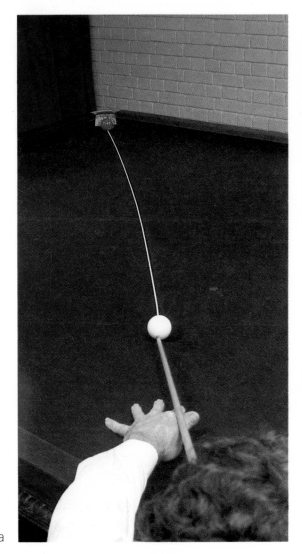

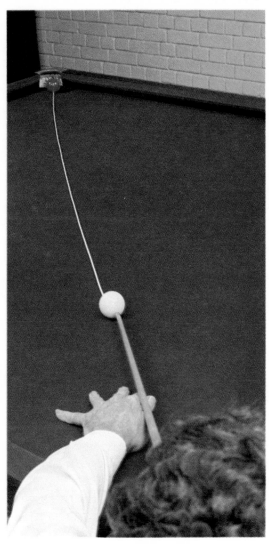

52a

52b

Off-centre Striking

52a and 52b indicate what happens to the cue ball when side is used. Compensating factors have to be taken into account when aiming. This knowledge develops with experience, *but side must always be respected and only used when necessary.*

52a shows the effect on the cue ball of lefthand side.

52b shows the effect on the cue ball of righthand side.

53

Practice in Cue Ball Control With Off-centre Striking and Compensation Factors in Aiming

Place three reds in line between the corner and centre pockets with the centre red on the pink spot as shown. Play the cue ball from the same position for each shot in the first sequence to pot three reds and four blacks (you start with the black).

1. Pot black with slight check side (lefthand in this case). *This will give position below the pink spot to pot the first red and secure position for the next black. If you can complete the sequence with all the reds in the lefthand corner pocket you are doing very well. Note the slight alteration of aim on the black to allow for off-centre cue ball striking. Cue smoothly and strike the horizontal centre of the cue ball with just the slightest hint of lefthand side.*

54

2. Pot black with screw and side. Each of the three reds is to be potted into the righthand centre pocket. This is a similar shot to 1 (above) but with more severe screw effect. Strike the cue ball low and slightly left of centre. Cueing should be crisp but not too hard. Note the different aim on the black.

55

3. Pot black with strong righthand side. *This is a difficult one, but learn from it. The reds are to be potted into the lefthand corner pocket. Very strong righthand side is required, striking right of the horizontal centre. Smooth and free* *cueing is essential to apply sufficient side to the cue ball. Note the off-pocket aim of the black; this will vary according to your ability to control the push-off of the cue ball with side and power. In other words quality of cueing.*

70

Some Half-ball Practice Shots

Half-ball shots are most useful and informative in practice and in general play. A 'half-ball' aim means that with centre cue ball striking the cue is aimed exactly at the edge of the object ball (it is therefore aimed at *half a ball's* width from the centre of the object ball). The sighting, because of its more positive nature, adds a little confidence to the player. Not only will you see exactly your line of aim to get the pot, but when succeeding, you will also be able to observe the angle or path that the cue ball takes after contact with the object ball for positional purposes, which is what success at the game is all about.

To pot consistently is proof of a good cue action. To pot a ball and put the cue ball in the correct position for the next stroke, give or take a little, demands quality of cueing and correct ball-to-ball contact. The most useful and interesting way to practise this is to pot the colours off their spots from the half-ball positions. So often do these shots appear in actual play that recognition of them develops quicker improvement. If you have the facilities to practise alone, play the half-ball shots in a repetitive fashion to impress the mind so that once learned never forgotten.

56–58 show the half-ball positions marked from cushion to ball but in order not to confuse you with too many lines, I have left the cue ball after-positions for your completion. Note that the well-executed stroke to pot the pink from the half-ball position (58) will not only pot it but also go in-off in the middle pocket, off the side cushion.

Natural In-offs

I have been amazed at the number of players who are not aware of the dangers of natural in-offs when going for a pot. In these days when billiards is played only by a comparative few, the pot in snooker has become rather a one-track journey and many of the skills of recognising natural in-offs, which are the billiard player's stock in trade, are, I fear, being lost.

When playing down the table against the nap, you must be aware of the drift of the object ball if played too slowly. Experiment and you will see what I mean.

I feel compelled to mention that in all these potting positions, the object is success through sound cueing at controlled pace, not to see or hear the object ball hit the back of the pocket

Understanding Billiards and Snooker

with a resounding smack at 100 m.p.h.
The sooner you realise that forcing shots
magnify any faults you may have, the
sooner your improvement will follow.
Habits are created, so form the right ones
from the beginning.

Half-ball Aim Practice Shots

*Photograph 56. Get to know these three
half-ball potting positions with black,
pink, and blue on their spots. When
cueing keep looking through the line of
aim.*

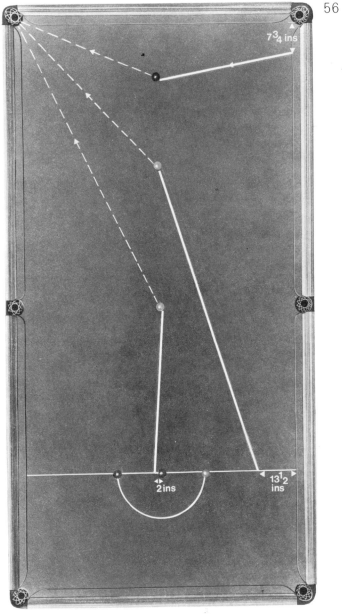

56

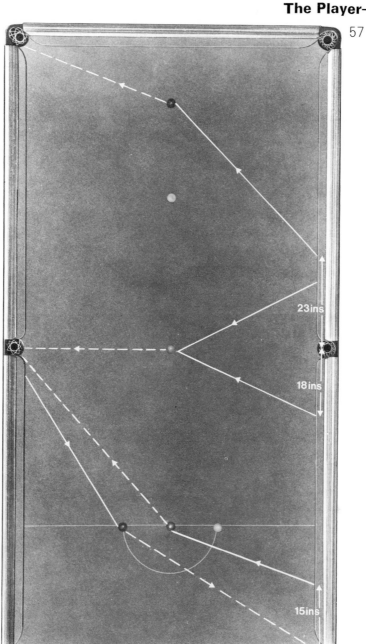

*57 and 58. Some more half-ball aim
shots to pot the colours off their spots.
Well worth remembering.*

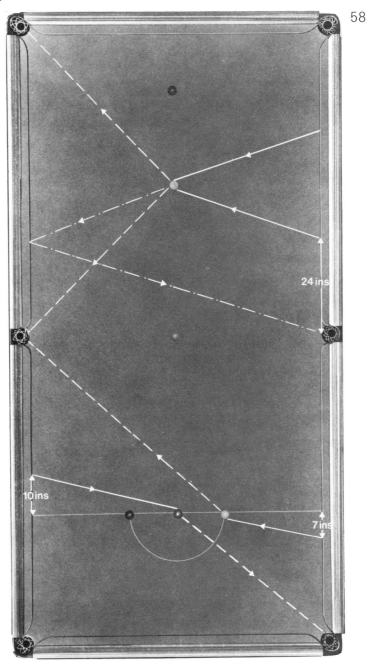

Timing and Co-ordination

Perhaps the most vital parts of technique but certainly the most difficult to put into words. Unlike stance, bridge hands, or cue holds, where the correct position of the feet, or fingers can be accurately described (and photographed), timing and co-ordination are concerned with rhythm, flow, or smoothness of movement combined with the maximum intensity of mental and physical effort.

In some sports timing and co-ordination in play are easy to recognise—the perfect leg glance or late cut in cricket, which by deft touch of the bat sends the ball flashing to the boundary; or the knockout punch in boxing which travels no more than a few inches. In billiards and snooker that little bit of magic the good player imparts to the cue ball is achieved by timing and co-ordination. When these are not right then there is little magic to be seen in the shots calling for side, screw, stun, or follow-through.

So timing and co-ordination exist as a part and the most important part of every shot you play; when you walk into your shot, take up your stance, and have your cue on the line of aim, you begin to co-ordinate your mental and physical efforts, adding the rhythm of the cue's backward and forward movement to your total concentration—even dedication—to the shot to be played, until you reach *that precise moment of time* when everything you are putting into the shot flows from you through the cue to the cue ball. Your concentration holds your head down firmly until your follow-through action is complete—and the stroke is successfully achieved.

Timing and co-ordination are personal things. They vary from one individual to another. An action that is too quick for one is too slow for another. Generally the beginner 'lets go' his shot *before* he has reached maximum intensity and efficiency in his preamble, and when his timing is bad it shows in the awkwardness or jerkiness of the stroke as well as in the pot that is missed.

For myself I know that if I delay my strike too long after I have looked at the object ball for the last time, or strike before I have given myself time to be composed, then the shot will probably be missed. Whenever I begin to feel I am not in form I look first to my timing and usually find the answer there. When you are playing at the top of your form your timing and co-ordination will be right, and every shot will feel sweet and smooth. Get to recognise the balanced rhythm that creates such a feeling and strive for it in every shot.

The eyes play an important role in the build-up to the stroke. When sighting through the object ball for the last time you have prepared yourself to strike, you have committed yourself physically— you should then play the shot with confidence—while your eyes will continue to hold you on the line of aim. At no time during the 'count-down' period to the shot can you afford to let your concentration lapse. You can be perfectly set to play when somebody may distract your attention by a cough, or by lighting a cigarette. This distraction breaks your rhythm, and you miss the stroke. The deeper you delve into the question of concentration the more you seem to come back to the basic requirements : if your technique is good and your preparation for the shot is good, one will help the other. You feel right,

you have confidence in yourself, and as this promotes good concentration, distractions will have less affect on you. Timing and co-ordination are linked to concentration, and underlying these are all the other elements of technique.

Good timing and co-ordination in play will inevitably show more in some people than others. It happens in all sports. Perhaps the best advice I can give you is this—understand what is meant by timing and co-ordination, understand their importance to your game of billiards or snooker—but acquire them by paying attention to all the other elements of technique I have described, and by playing every shot with confidence. Good timing and co-ordination will be the natural result of your mastery of the more definable parts of technique—it is rare indeed to find it happening the other way round.

Preparation for Every Shot

Let us now put together in words all the things that will establish a methodical approach for every shot creating a set of good habits for your future play.

Place a red ball approximately 12 in. from the side cushion and 24 in. from the top cushion. From hand we have a series of pots by placing the cue ball anywhere in the 'D'. Having set your shot up you have what can be your imaginary 'leave'.

(1) Stand behind the shot studying the position and make your decision and plan of intention.

(2) Step forward into your stroke and with care place your feet astride the shot, remembering to remain in the standing position, judging your balance and poise and distance from the shot.

(3) When you are satisfied with your position bend into the shot placing your bridge hand into position—do this quite unhurriedly and concentrate hard on your line of aim, addressing the cue ball where you intend to strike, letting your eyes look back and forth from well behind the bridge hand along the cue right through the shot. This is most important. If you find that your cue is on line without any need to sway the body then your feet placement has been correct. If not then a slight fidgetting of the feet is necessary to put your cue on line.

(4) Having now settled into your shot, finally look at the object ball through the line of aim, stay there and play your shot in your own time. If you will forgive the repetition, it is this sequence of events that one has to co-ordinate with sighting to produce that smooth rhythm which is timing.

The Expert's Approach

Each stroke in a snooker break is really a break within itself, unlike billiards where the flow of the break and the run of the shots become more rhythmic. In billiards a good player is looking farther ahead anyway, and is almost expecting the next position to arrive. In snooker the first essential is to get the pot and the second is to achieve position. If the pot fails, then you have to wait until you can start again with the same thing in mind. I think in this respect the expert has a far sounder approach to every shot he plays than the average player, who will be so pleased at getting his shot, getting a chance to play, that he hurries to the table and seeing the ball he wants to pot he gets down very quickly, shuffles his feet into position, away goes the pot, and he either scores or he does not !

The expert will approach the table smoothly. He will stand back from the shot, then walk into it from maybe a couple of paces right behind the line, put his feet into position, concentrating and *virtually playing the shot from the standing or half-standing position*. He then eases his body down into the shot and when he gets down he finds that invariably he is bang on line, whereas often the club player when he gets down will have to sway his body or shuffle a little to get into position. It is this fact which creates so much havoc when delivering the cue because the movement created by the stroke sways the body back to its original position which was incorrect. The expert does not allow this fundamental error in stance to creep into his game. You will rarely see him shuffle his feet once he is down—he is pretty well right the first time. This approach to the table before you play the shot is so terribly important.

I have spoken to and coached so many players that I find it difficult to get this message across even in personal coaching. It is just not appreciated how difficult this game is, and how important it is to search and struggle for every grain of help that can be obtained before committing yourself to the shot.

If you find that my insistence on proper attention to all the elements of technique is giving you more to think about than you would like and giving you problems you did not know even existed, do understand that to find it out for yourself can take a lifetime, so be patient. Your timing is personal, do not try to copy any player you may admire for speed of play. Do what is right for you. If your technique is sound it will hold you together on the stroke and remember, you are never going to get them all so do not grumble too much when you miss and feel you should not have done. Make sure you try to do better next time.

Touch

Many players have told me that they wish they had a better touch. If I can be the guinea pig let me tell you what I have found in my own play. In the first place I hit the ball very hard yet I am able to play the most delicate of cannons, soft screws, and nurseries when they present themselves. Touch should not be confused with ball contact. In delicate stroke-play contact is extremely important in controlling the speed and distance that the cue ball will travel. Touch is the sweetness of your delivery and the perfection of your timing. So once again we see how one element of technique is so dependent on others.

As a player makes progress in the game he will find his timing will improve and he may notice this more with one shot than another. The good player gets his cue through the shot in his delivery, follow-through if you like, and he leaves his cue there on the shot instead of snatching it back or away from the shot. Perhaps you have seen the expert carpenter drive a nail into a piece of wood in such an easy way, yet when you try to do the same you tighten your muscles, have a whack, and the nail does not go in anything like as far. In snooker touch is the result of timing and quality of action and follow-through. Endeavour and enthusiasm while essential are no substitutes for the timing and quality of action that the expert has acquired.

An Exercise in Touch
Put a ball tight on the cushion anywhere, place the cue ball 4 in. away on the table and practise for a few minutes with little kiss shots controlling the distance of the kiss-back within the 4 in. Try also to develop a rhythm as you play this exercise to build a succession of strokes in well-balanced time.

Softness when holding the butt is of paramount importance. I find that, when I play in hot conditions and my butt hand is moist, the cue literally sticks to my hand and almost completely eliminates the need for the normal hold. It is then that I find soft screw and delicate shots can be so easily and sweetly achieved.

Mastery in the use of your cue will, with regular practice, open up a host of shots and positional possibilities. Touch in the quality player is something we can all see and appreciate—but touch is not easy to acquire. The more you play, the more your touch *should* improve—but only if you make yourself deliberately conscious of the effects you are

79

achieving. I place touch very high in the list of priorities for success, and as it cannot happen by accident, give it all the attention it deserves.

Tactics

A few words on tactics. To give advice to anybody about to play an important match and by that I mean at any level, is easy enough. It will no doubt be good advice but it depends whether the player concerned can, or wants to, listen and be guided at such a crucial time. It is so easy to score goals for England at Wembley from an armchair in front of the television. So perhaps the best advice I can give you is to present yourself in a relaxed state of mind, being as normal as possible. It is at these times when you should welcome the opportunity to try out all the things you have put into your practice and games. It is no use at all practising one method and playing another for fear it may not work and cost you the result..I repeat, the one thing about sound technique is to give you strength when pressure is around. Ask any champion at international level.

Of course temperament comes into the game tremendously and one can only say to the more sensitive man—try to relax and put it together. If you can do it at other times, why not now ? The game of snooker by its very tactical nature allows temperament to play a more vital part than many other sports and games. However, if a player is keen enough and goes looking for matches he will become much less susceptible to the nervous excitement that the annual championship match at this club may have created formerly.

I have always tried to make the game my only competitor, and always sought to achieve artistic perfection, content to win in my turn. But the world looks for winners and it's their names that can be sure of a place in the record books. In all sport where winning is the sole objective gamesmanship creeps in but my experience has been that people who resort to unsporting methods do so because of their lack of ability to win by fair means. Be honest and let your skills and integrity speak for you.

Adopt a positive attitude to the game. When you have decided on your shot play it with confidence and play your safety shots with the same care as you do your pots and never avoid the opportunity of a shot to nothing if that is the way out of trouble. Snooker at its best is when played as an attacking game. Don't become a hit and run player all the time if you really want to improve. Too much safety can put you on the defensive and get your state of mind the same, and even inspire your opponent to more confident moods. Concentrate 100% when it is your turn, relax when you are sitting out but pay attention to your opponent and his play. You may learn something. Do not grudge him his luck when he gets it. Hope that your turn will come and above all if you lose take it with a smile even though it hurts. In the end you will appreciate your victories all the more.

The Nap

The nap of the cloth running from the baulk end to the top end of the table does have an effect on the strokes you play with side and screw. A new or thick nap will exaggerate the effect of both. Likewise an old or worn cloth will show less effect. The experienced player will try to adjust accordingly and temper his judgement to the conditions involved. Wet or humid conditions tend to lessen the effects of screw and side on the bed of the table but not necessarily from the surface of the cushions. Warm, dry conditions will ensure lively screw and spin effects and resilient cushions. These are undoubtedly the best conditions to play under.

Strokes against the nap should be played where possible without side or at a pace that will not allow the nap to have any effect on the cue ball in its path to the object ball. The action against the nap is to reverse the effects of side on the path of the cue ball when played too slowly, and can have a slight effect even on fairly long fast shots. The slow shot will not come back on to the line after the initial push-off but continues to drift away from the normal curve and when slowing down will positively pull in the opposite direction from the normal as long as it has spin. With the fast shot the same thing happens to an extremely fine limit that is not easy to discern. These effects can be used to advantage by expert players, but until such time as the standard of your play has developed to a satisfactory level, centre ball striking is essential when playing against the nap.

Wearing Spectacles

Players of all standards often ask me about spectacles for playing. I have experimented quite a lot and have found the most satisfactory type is a frame made with a low bridge which raises the lens slightly on the face. The lenses should be fairly large or deep and fitted with a nylon cord in place of the top rim. These two factors will give you clear vision when down on the shot.

The sides should have a fixed angle to suit the individual and to hold the front piece snug to the face. Swivel joints on the sides do not stay constant due to wear and can be very irritating when in play. Make sure the ear-pieces or side ends fit well and are longer than normal spectacles round the ears to ensure a constant hold and to prevent them from slipping down the nose.

The lenses should be de-centred if necessary to the correct pupillary distance so that you get no distortion when in the playing position. When I see players who enjoy the game playing in their everyday heavy-rimmed spectacles, which will invariably cause distortion or obscure the vision in play because of the unnatural position that the head is in, I wonder how they play at all. Newcomers to glasses have to be patient and strong-willed to overcome the initial strangeness. Brightness and glare may cause concern but perseverance will overcome these things.

Lightness in weight is also important. If you need to have large lenses, which may or may not be thick, it can help to have plastic ones which are considerably lighter in weight. Having been actively employed in the family business of manufacturing opticians all my life, the advice I have given here is professional in every sense of the word, and will provide you with the specification for good billiard spectacles.

As I have said before the game itself is difficult enough so do not give yourself the added handicap of seeing furry or oval balls. If you need glasses for playing then get the right ones and see for yourself the difference they make !

The 'Jack Karnehm' Billiard Spectacles

I personally produced this hand-made spectacle frame shown here to illustrate the essential requirements of bridge height, rimless top, fixed side angle, and deep ear pieces. The actual measurements will vary for the individual.

Part Three
SNOOKER

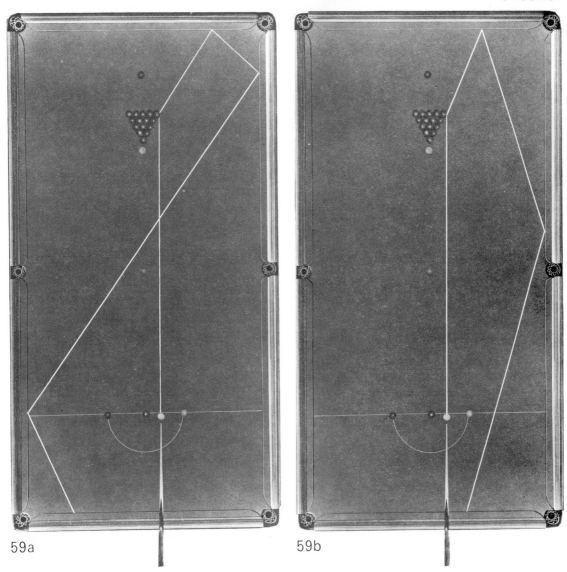

59a

59b

The Opening Shot

1. Strike the top outside red with righthand side (59A). Remember to make a very slight allowance for the push-away of the cue ball. The inclination is to push the cue ball into the reds making too thick a contact. Smooth cueing is essential.

2. The safer break when under tension (59B), or when you are not so expert, is a plain ball stroke with the cue ball making thin contact on the last outside red (as in 1). An excellent safety position can follow as a result of correct pace and contact.

85

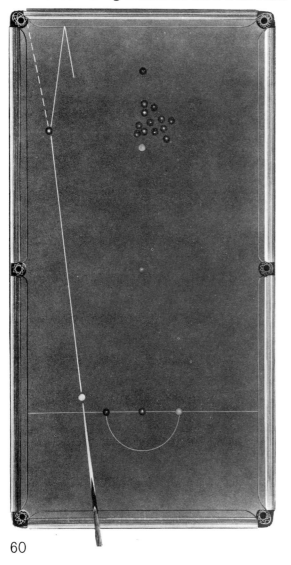

60

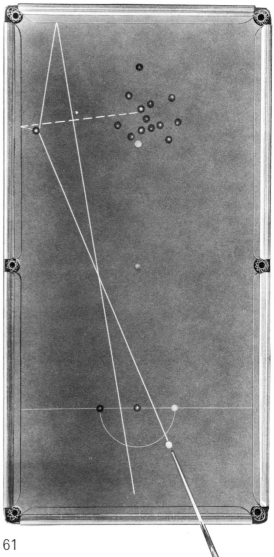

61

The Time to Have A Go (60)

A typical position at the beginning of a game when there are no loose reds. Play for the pot, be positive and confident; this is sound technique.

When to Play Safe (61)

With the white in this position the pot is difficult and chancy. It is far better to play a careful half-ball shot off the red to leave your opponent in a really unpleasant position.

86

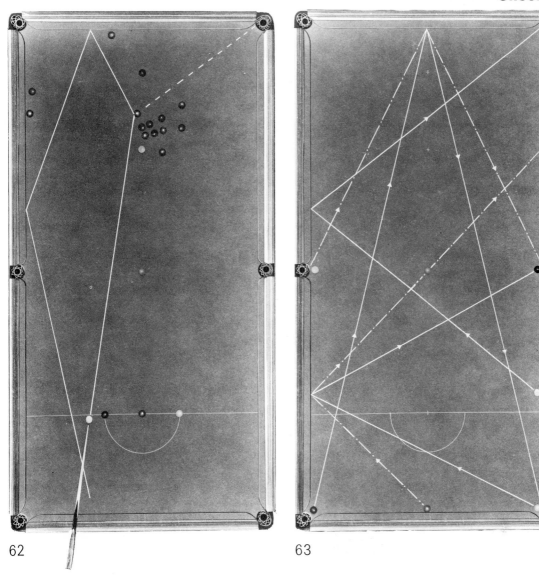

62

63

A Shot to Nothing (62)

Take no chances. Try to pot the possible red with safety in mind making sure the cue ball returns to a safe position even if the pot is successful. Discretion is the better part of valour and any snooker laid for your opponent is never pleasant for him. This shot needs a slight touch of check side (righthand in this case) to

ensure good clearance of the side reds.

Angles of Incidence (63)

A ball played on to a cushion at normal pace without side will come off the cushion it strikes at an angle equal to that which it approached. 63 shows some of the fairly obvious angles—get to know them!

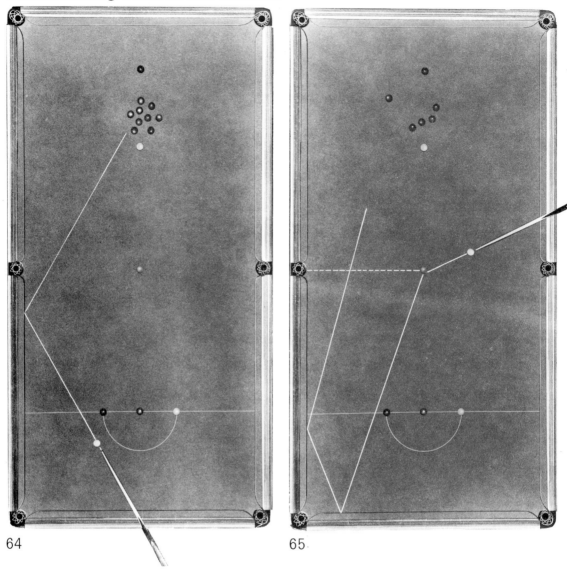

64

65

An Angle to Remember (64)

Snookered on all the reds: note the point of aim to the cushion. It's surprising how often this simple-looking angle is misjudged and points given away.

A Position to Remember (65)

When close to a half-ball pot on the blue, the cue ball will just miss the corner of the 'D' and the corner pocket.

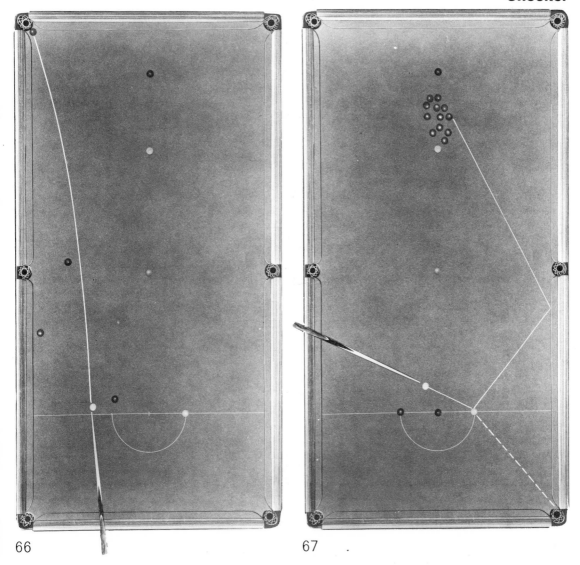

66   67

A Simple Swerve (66)

To pot the red when just snookered play with lefthand side and slightly raise the cue butt. This will swerve the cue ball as shown.

A Shot Worth Cultivating (67)

Pot yellow with screw and a little lefthand side to bring the cue ball into the pack. This shot can be played off any baulk colour in a similar position, and is not as difficult as it looks.

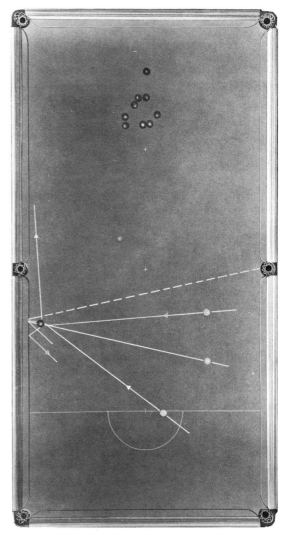

68

Doubles—Three Angles for the Same Pocket (68)

The cross-double is indicated by the lines with the solid arrows. Be careful to avoid the kiss with the object ball coming back from the side cushion. Aim to hit righthand side of the object ball.

The straight double is indicated by the plain line. Probably easier than the other two doubles shown because it is a 'natural' angle.

The reverse double is shown with the clear arrows. Here it is half-ball aim on the lefthand side of the object ball.

69

Break-building Shots

1. A 'set' in the pack (69). *Keep watch for this typical plant. Sets can easily go unobserved in the heat of the moment, but they offer a chance to open the reds a little and get on a colour. In playing this shot the ball 'on' was potted. The third ball in the set dislodged the two reds near the black enough to leave more easy points.*

70

2. Pot the pink and open the reds (70). *Another typical position on the pink offering the opportunity for break building. Play a crisp shot with top* *striking to pot the pink, open the reds a little and keep the cue ball in the clear off the near red.*

3. Slow screw—when to cannon (71).
Play this shot with low-striking and no side. Note the narrow pocket entrance making accuracy essential. In order to stay nicely on the black gently cannon on to the two reds. This is a good touch stroke to master.

72

4. Slow screw—when not to cannon
(72). *Strike the cue ball low with
righthand side compensating this with
off-pocket aim. The red will be thrown to
the centre of the pocket, and the thicker
contact on the red takes the pace from
the cue ball. This is a break-building shot
for the better player, keeping a tight
control on the cue ball.*

5. Pot black and make a red to follow
(73). *With the reds still tightly bunched
do not try to smash the pack when
potting this black. It is better to play a
crisp shot to clip the outside red. This is
more likely to leave something to follow.*

73

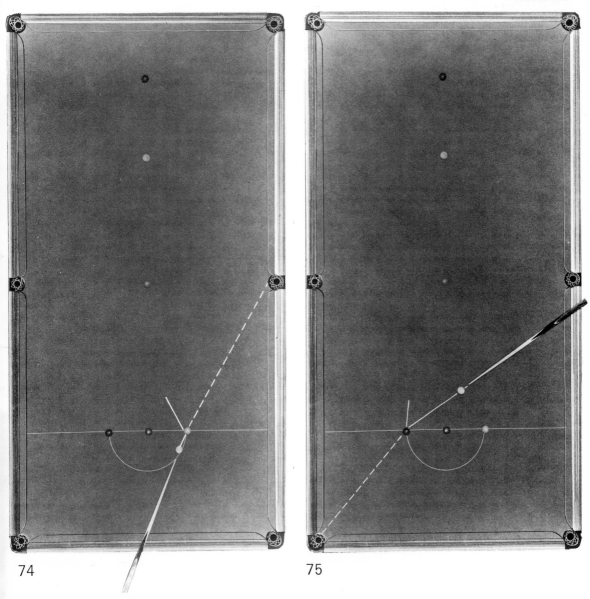

74

75

Potting the Colours Off Their Spots—Starting From the 'D' and Not Using the Cushions

1. Yellow (74). *Pot at an angle into the centre pocket to give a natural line on the green.*

2. Green (75). *A delicate screw not allowing the cue ball any forward movement. This will ensure a fairly straight line on the brown.*

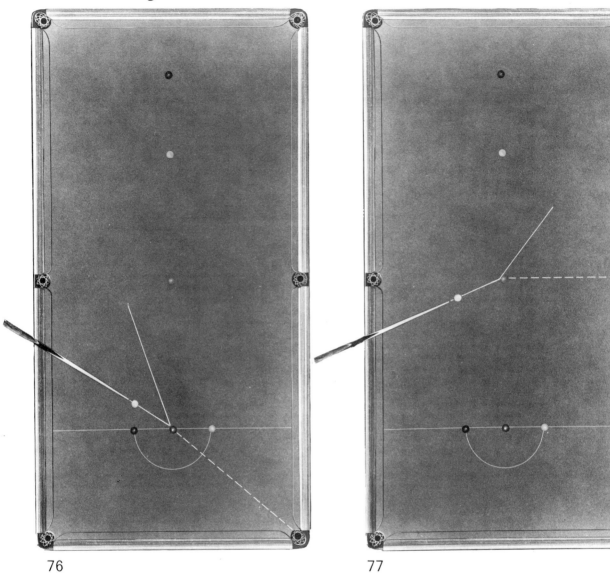

76

77

3. Brown (76). *A nicely timed fairly deep screw with not too much wrist in this shot. Keep as close as possible to the line from the blue to the middle pocket taking care not to go above it.*

4. Blue (77). *A thick pot on the blue to help cue ball control. Take care not to overshoot the line for potting pink into the top corner pocket.*

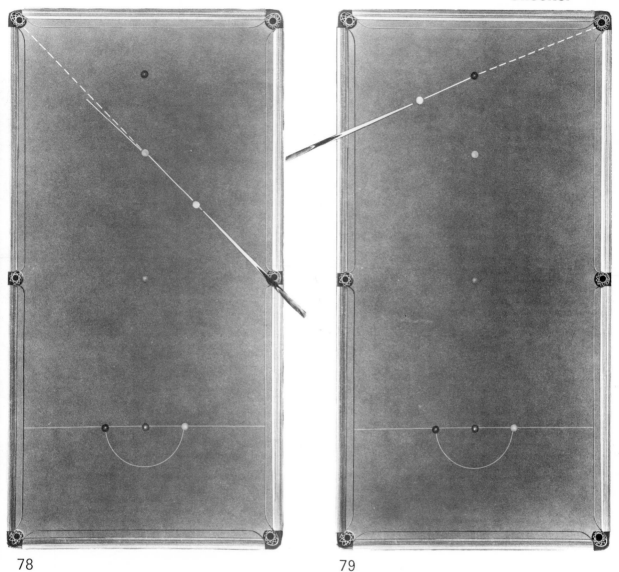

78

79

5. Pink (78). *Pot the pink with centre cue ball striking. Dead strength is needed for position on the black.*

6. Black (79). *In this case sight through the middle with crisp and accurate striking just below centre.*

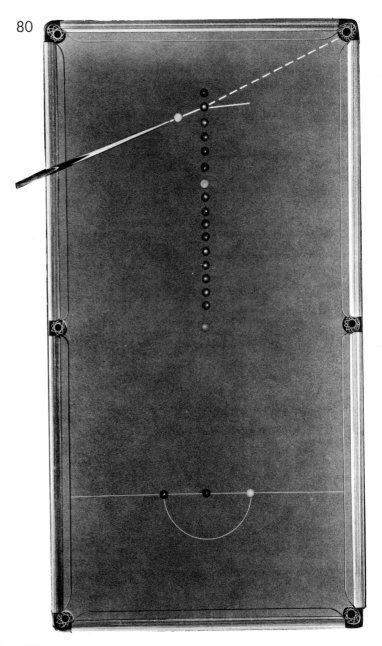

An Interesting Set Practice Piece (80)

With the colours on their spots and the reds placed as shown, pot a red then a colour in any order without disturbing the set in any way. Count your breaks. End by potting the colours off their spots.

Part Four
BILLIARDS

Development of the Game

Billiards began to take its place in our society as a pleasant pastime around the 1820s. Tables were then pretty crude. Cushions were stuffed with a sort of calico and horse-hair, and had little resilience if any at all. Even the early rubber cushions would 'freeze' in cold weather never to regain their original elasticity. Balls were made of ivory and behaved very differently from today's.

Jonathon (Edwin) Kentfield was the first professional to exploit the game but it was not until John Roberts, Senior, in 1850 and 1860 that the game really began to get public notice. Subsequently John Roberts, Junior, became quite a famous professional and dominated the 1870s and 1880s. From then on the game produced some very fine professional billiards players and it went through a phase of competitive play that produced magnificent feats in terms of large breaks, all developed on various principles of repetitive play, with, of course, their own forms of variations calling for the highest possible skills.

By the 1930s the game had been exploited to the full and the rules were changed to try to control the breaks that the great Walter Lindrum had shown were possible. To his credit he overcame all such efforts to limit breaks and continued to make thousand breaks in spite of all the restrictions that were imposed.

I think it is worth noting that the rules are more restricting today than they were in those days, and even then many people believed that the restrictions were killing the game. However, this state of affairs has existed from the days of Tom Newman when thousand breaks were made to empty houses. The same arguments prevailed then as they do today. Perhaps this is the wrong approach if survival of the game is genuinely desired.

Billiards is still being played all over the world, particularly in Commonwealth countries. Who knows, perhaps we have seen the complete cycle now and should completely remove the playing restrictions to create new interest, and to develop the game and all its skills again, and then take an enlightened view on the value of re-introducing scoring limitations once this has been achieved.

The Beauty of Billiards

The snooker player can learn so much from billiards and the knowledge will improve his snooker beyond his belief. Both games are very much complementary to each other, and for the enthusiast nothing can be more refreshing and conducive to good play than a little variation.

I have helped and coached many very good amateur snooker players who have been amazed to see in billiards, shots they did not know were possible or how the desired effects were achieved, so I hope I can whet your appetite for just some of the beautiful shots played in billiards.

When you can play billiards well, recognising angles and ball contacts ; understanding the subtle differences in positional play that side and screw can offer ; appreciating the infinite variety of strokes played so delicately, then you will be able to play any game on a billiards table. A good billiards player will always play snooker well, but the reverse is not necessarily the case.

Snooker played at top level is a wonderful game, terribly demanding in accuracy and technique of delivery. It is a game of short duration when players can lose frames but eventually win the match. The run of the balls has more say in snooker adding to its charm and popularity. It is a game of excitement for the average player ; he can handicap his play with any opponent and spice it a little more with a side stake.

Billiards, on the other hand, is characterised by more fluency in play with longer periods of continuous concentration. The tremendous variation in play and strokes demands quite a different approach and playing technique from snooker. In a game using only three balls, unless you have a fairly sound method of retaining position, the scoring breaks for the average player can be few and far between. The accuracy demanded for in-off play is not as great as that for potting in terms of actually getting the shot, but the positional factor is far more critical in order to continue a break in a fluent way. Should you miss the position you played for you will not find several other balls 'on' and it can be extremely difficult to maintain the break.

In a billiards handicap, the superior skill of the better player will keep the game a one-sided affair, and unless the handicap is so heavy as to make a slight nonsense of playing, the better player will nearly always win a serious game.

However, billiards and snooker do

Understanding Billiards and Snooker

have one thing in common—both are extremely difficult to play well.

It is inconceivable that such a beautiful game as billiards could be lost to the player who has the skill and dedication required to play and who derives such satisfaction from it. As the younger generations come along they only play snooker because they have no one to show them the skills of billiards to any degree. It will be a sad day if we ever have to talk of billiards as the game that was.

Top of the Table Play

It would be an arduous but pleasant task to write a complete thesis on billiards but in this book I must be as explicit as possible in my choice of subject matter from the game trusting that it will entice enthusiasts to delve a little deeper into some of the more sophisticated methods of play in search of all-round improvement. I have yet to meet the snooker player who would not benefit from having a reasonable working knowledge of billiards.

In my first book on billiards and snooker I linked a number of billiard in-off (or losing hazard) shots together as the basis for continuous play, or break building, demanding a smooth cue action without which there is little hope of real success for anyone.

Now let us look at the top of the table play where the discerning snooker player can improve his knowledge and skills to overcome the 30 break story of his life. Some might say that to put balls in position and make a break is useless unless you can get them there in actual play. Well, that is fair criticism, but Rome was not built in a day, and any hard practice combined with an understanding of purpose is beneficial. With reasonable skills you can play the balls into the required position anyway, as I will explain later.

The quickest way to understand top of the table play is to select a sequence of shots and practise them until a repetitive method is at your command, you have acquired the right touch, and are playing the strokes well.

I hope that readers who have followed my last book will have developed their all-round play and acquired a cue action that will permit some intense practice play around the spot end.

The sequence I have chosen is a 10-break series of pot red and cannon. It should be noted that I have not included repetitive potting off the spot, as only two consecutive pots are now allowed off the spot after which the red is placed on the centre spot unless a cannon intervenes.

Pay extreme care to touch with the cannon play trying to keep close control of the balls ; be aware of thick and thin contacts for controlling the pace of the cue and object balls. So often a red can be potted by thick or thin contacts to give varying positions for the cue ball. Use whichever is suitable to gain every possible advantage for your next shot.

Think in advance with your shots.

Understanding Billiards and Snooker

Practice will soon make you aware of this fact. The sequence I have played in this method I have played a thousand times. Adjustment to each stroke to maintain position for the next shot is the key to success. *Improvisation is the art of trying to maintain perfection.*

The Guide for Position

You will see in the photographs that the table is marked with guide lines to explain the method and top of the table position we tried to achieve. The space behind the red marked X is where not to place the opponent's white during this particular sequence. The extreme side lines of the box are the approximate limit that you should allow the object ball to escape from the spot. The line

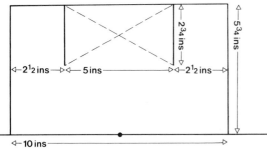

Figure 4. Top of the table box

across the whole width of the table (drawn through the billiard spot 12¾ in. from the top cushion) is the guide for positioning your cue ball in relation to the next shot. To perform the exercise correctly you must employ a sufficient degree of control to get the cue ball back down the table, crossing this main line after every pot red you play.

This is not so demanding when practised by the good player. Always

remember to concentrate on this imaginary line and the strength of the shot required to get the cue ball to cross it rather than to worry continually where your cue ball must or should stop. This helps to dispel confusion from the mind. *Strength is something you play. If applied correctly when scoring, your next position is automatic as often as not.*

When the object white is close to the boundary line, a cannon should be played coming under the object white from the top cushion with enough strength to push it on to or near the main line, trying not to cross it. This is the key stroke to the method and the strength and accuracy will depend to a large extent on contact with the red. A thick contact will slow the pace of the cue ball thereby permitting a certain freedom of delivery, whereas a thin contact will allow more pace in the cue ball, and less in the first object ball. These factors you must consider to control both object balls, while not forgetting direction. This return of the object white to the main line is of tremendous importance to recovery of the object white to its place behind the red. At all times the contact under the object white should be to send it within the space marked. This will prevent possible covers of the spot by the object white.

The sequence I have described is just one of many variations. All the time you will find yourself having to improvise or compensate in strength and contact to try to maintain position. Often you will make a complete mess of it. Keep persevering with accuracy in mind. Inventiveness will gradually creep into your play as your touch improves bringing with it more control. It is getting the touch for top of the table play that can be difficult. When this is achieved you will find many pretty shots and moves to maintain control of the white behind the spot.

Setting Up the Position

As we said at the start how to set up this top of the table situation is important. The desired position of the balls can be most easily achieved when you have two object balls in good positions near the middle pockets. Let us firstly take the obvious way, that is by going in off the white from hand and pushing the object white to a place behind the spot, then potting the red from hand and running the cue ball into position for a pot off the spot. Always ensure at the outset that the red is pottable and that the cue ball can be properly controlled in potting the red before you despatch the object white to the spot end.

In open play the cannon method is often on but not detected. Take the basic type of drop cannon, so named because all three balls are dropped, so to speak, at the top end of the table. From photograph 96 a slightly thicker than half-ball cannon off the white will gather the three balls together, sometimes well placed, sometimes not so well placed, for continuing the break. So again you have to improvise.

Perhaps a more certain method is to play your cannon from a slightly wider position with a little running side. Care should be taken not to strike below centre, driving the red to the far corner

pocket as shown in photograph 96 off the side cushion.

Photograph 95 shows a similar type of cannon with the red nearer the top corner pocket and the white object ball in a drop position. By playing correct strength and contact the white goes to the spot end and the red is knocked over the corner pocket for a shot to get top end position.

Contact on the second object ball in these cannons, in fact with any cannon, is extremely important. If you judge your angle correctly, and have placed your cue ball likewise, your concentration should be on the first object contact, which is very hard indeed, and you should not allow your cue to wander off the line by looking at the second object ball in anticipation of the result. At all times keep looking through the line of the shot.

Awareness of these types of shot opens up a variety of cannons to get your mind working. When playing from object white to object red always try to ensure that the second object ball, that is the red, is away from the top cushion. The reason for this is to allow the red to be pushed towards the pocket directly rather than bounced off the top cushion when it can so often be sent too far away and the position lost. The reverse is advisable from red to white. Try to land full on the white object ball to prevent a possible cover for the next shot on the red. At the pace these shots are played judgement of the correct thickness of contact is extremely important.

The majority of your shots in this method should be even-paced allowing smooth delivery of cue and accurate

Understanding Billiards and Snooker

striking of the cue ball. Positional play in general is an improvisation of shots to achieve theoretical perfection. When your breaks go so well that it all seems easy then beware not to take it for granted. It is just a glimpse of what is really possible and will spur you on in hopes of a longer taste the next time. This I have found a never-ending pattern and applies to both the billiards and the snooker player.

Top of the Table Sequence Without Repetitive Potting

The size of the box marked on the table

in the photographs illustrating this top of the table method is 10 in. × 5¾ in. The guide lines are 2¾ in. long and 2½ in. from each end of the box. The area in the box marked with an X in 87 shows where you should not leave the object white in this series of play because you must have space around the spot for re-spotting the red and avoiding covers.

Note very carefully the ball positions in relation to the lines in all shots played.
1. Cannon (81). *The red is on its spot and the object white at the top of the positional line. Play with very slight lefthand side on the cue ball, and thick contact on the red with just enough strength to reach the object white.*

81

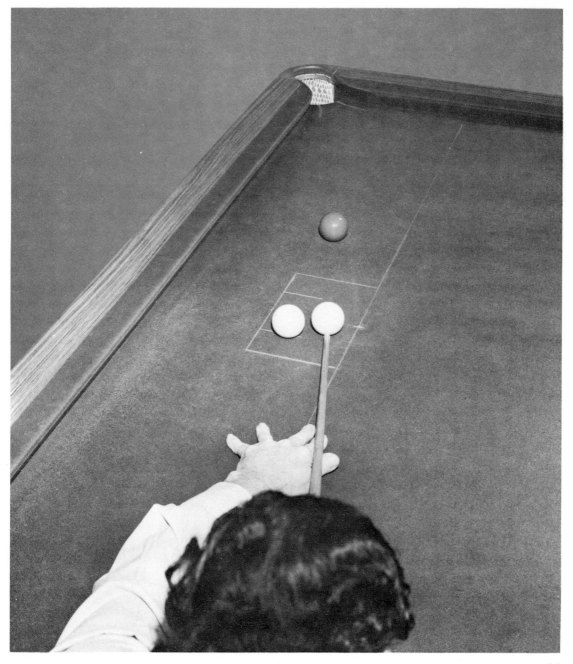

2. Pot red (82). *With stun and screw—a fairly straight-forward shot. The cue ball crosses the main line*

83

3. Pot red (83). *Off the spot. Play a crisp stun pot to leave the original position as in 81, but with the object white having moved only ¼ in. as can be seen from 84.*

84

4. A gentle cannon (84). *This time my touch is a little better (note the position of the red in 85).*

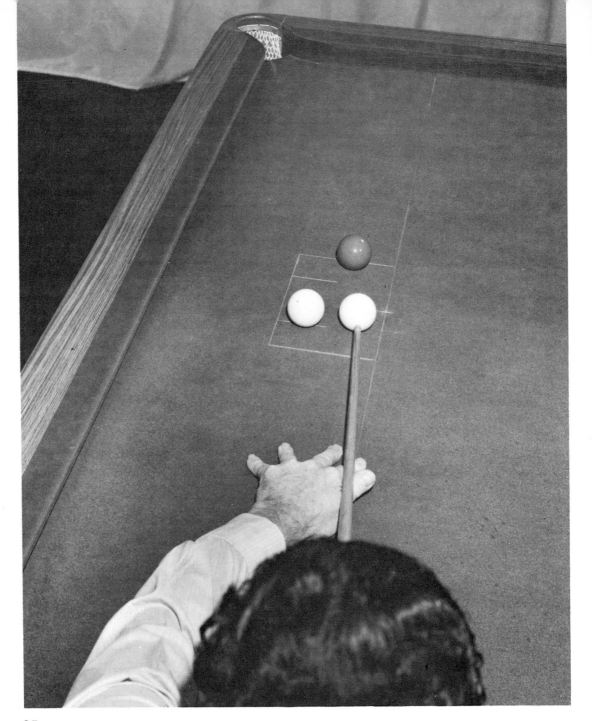

85

5. (85). *Let us assume that I have played another sequence and in doing so have pushed the object white to the edge of the box. I now pot the red bringing the cue ball a little lower down the table by stun and screw, not a difficult shot.*

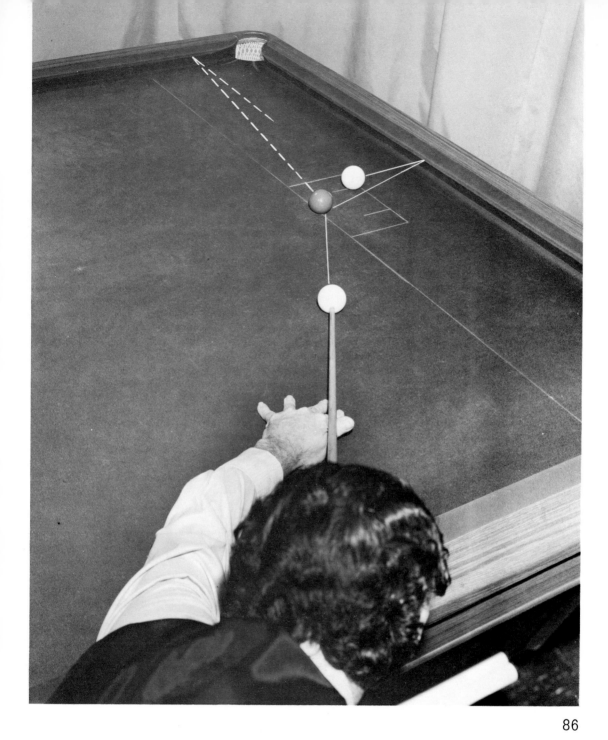

6. Cannon (86). *As indicated, play with just a touch of check (righthand in this case) side coming under the object white from the top cushion. Thick* *contact on the red gives pace to the red but takes it from the cue ball. A key shot* to practise.

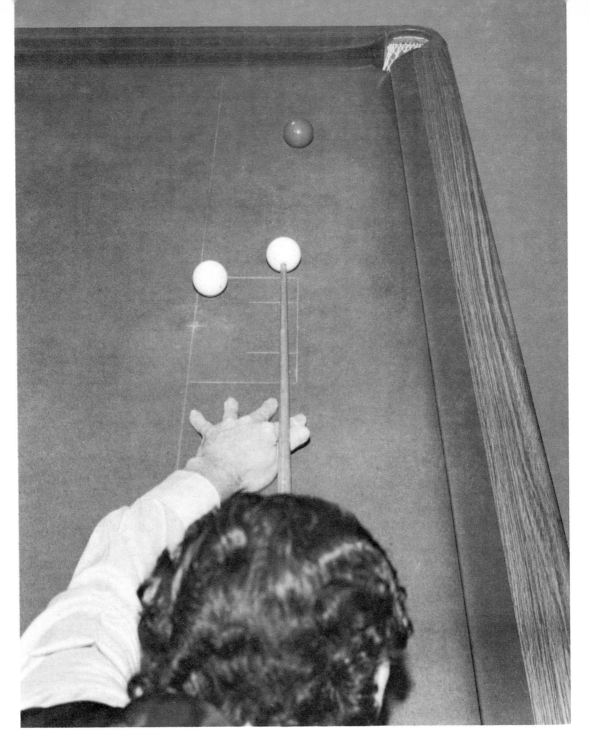

87

7. Pot red (87). *This is the position after playing the shot in 86. A simple shot that can be played freely because the* *object white is positioned in the box but almost on the main line, allowing a big margin of error for the cue ball.*

88

8. Cannon (88). *With the object white in this main line position play a thickish cannon gently off it so that the object white comes back from the top cushion to somewhere inside the box, preferably on the guide line.*

89

9. Pot red (89). *The position now obtained having played 8 allows you to continue the break. Try screwing back to leave position 1, or play a gentle stun shot to leave position 3.*

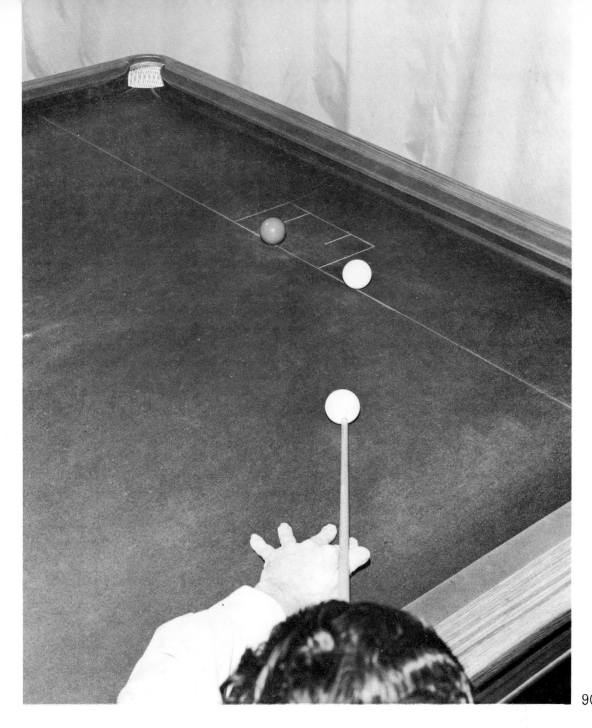

Top of the Table Play—'The Main Line' and the Position of the Object White

It is vitally important to keep the object white up to the line when it escapes

from the box as 90–91 show.

90. With the cue ball at some distance from the box an easy positional cannon is still possible to maintain the top of the table play in this method.

91

91. The cue ball is in the same position as in 90 but the loss of position of the object white now requires more demanding stroke play to maintain the sequence. Keep thinking two shots ahead.

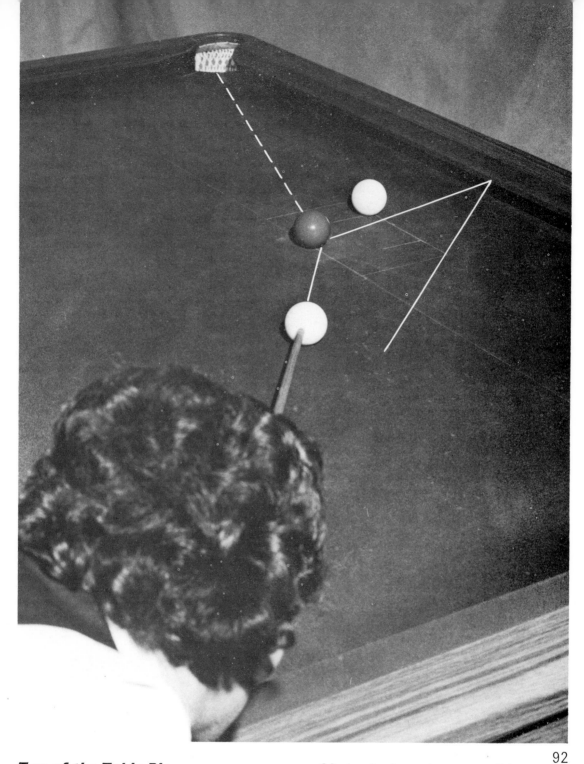

**Top of the Table Play—
Variations**

*92 clearly shows how a confident
potter can take extra pots before playing
the cannon (as in the 10-break series).*

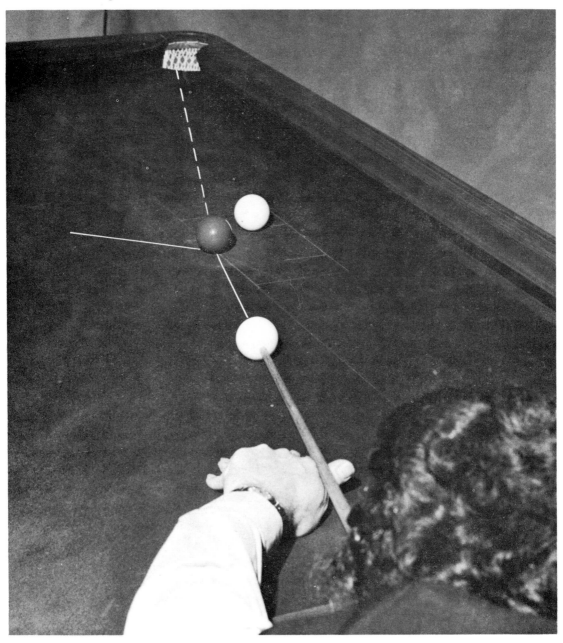

93

Under the previous rules, 93 shows the possibility of a pot red, running through gently to give a return pot. Then play a third pot to leave the cannon as indicated. Remember that under the present rules, after one pot off the spot the cannon must be played to keep the red on the billiard spot to maintain

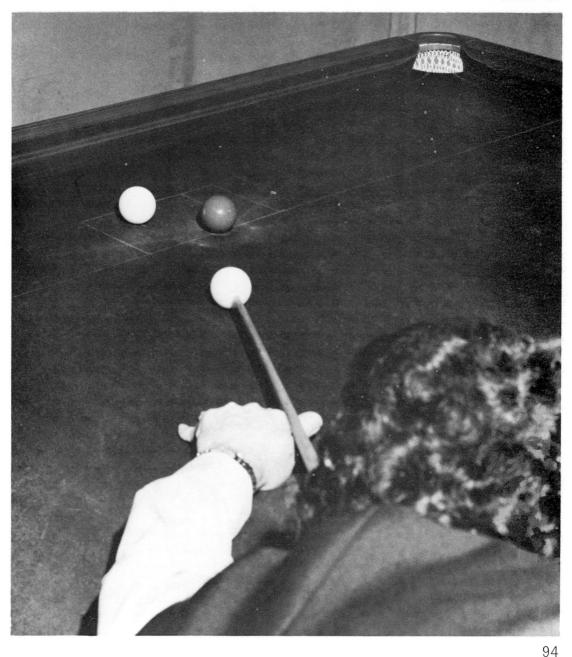

94

position for top of the table play, as only
two consecutive pots are now allowed
off the spot, when it is then placed on
the middle spot.

The position in 94 permits a gentle
cannon to give a position for resumed
potting before taking another cannon.

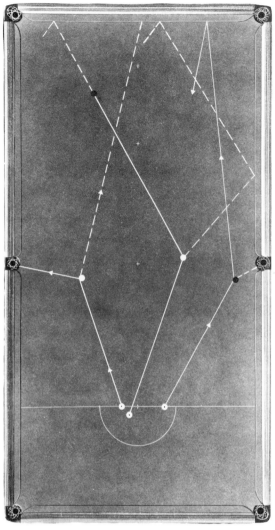

95

Approach Shots for Top of the Table Play

1. Three shots played from the 'D' (95). *The in-off white into the lefthand middle pocket, and the pot red into the righthand middle pocket clearly give you a top of the table position to follow.*

Before the white is sent to the spot end ensure that the red is a comfortable pot.
The cannon from white to red gives you a top of the table position in one shot. Contacts are extremely important in this cannon. Always try to keep the red in front of you.

120

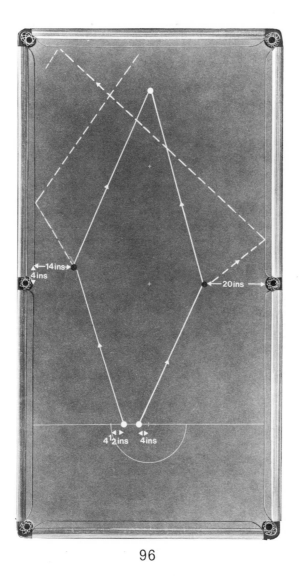

96

2. Two cannons played from the 'D' (96).
*The lefthand drop cannon from red to
white leaves the three balls at the top
end. Concentrate on first ball contact.*

*The righthand cannon from red to
white takes the red across to the top
corner pocket and leaves the white near*
*the billiard spot. This is a little more
certain than the drop cannon.*

121

Shots to Test Technique

Everyone has his pleasure in shot making. Billiards and snooker provide an endless variety of shots that give the performer and onlooker as much pleasure as any other form of entertainment. Many is the time I have been round a table with the local enthusiasts discussing the rights and wrongs and have been surprised at some of the shots that Bill or Fred came out with, much to their joy when they succeeded. These moments leave memories and create a talking point that lasts over the years, and the longer the discussions go on the harder the shots seem to get. To the serious player this is the lighter side of the game that provides the relaxation so necessary after a session of extreme tension or hard practice, when players and onlookers can talk on the stroke without fear of the roof falling in on their heads.

I would like to show you how to play a few advanced shots, not trick shots. I have made these into a routine pastime to help in my cueing and technique, with the added advantage of giving a little pleasure should anyone be watching. These shots demand considerably more expertise than the general run of shots, but when mastered give a feeling of confidence and good form.

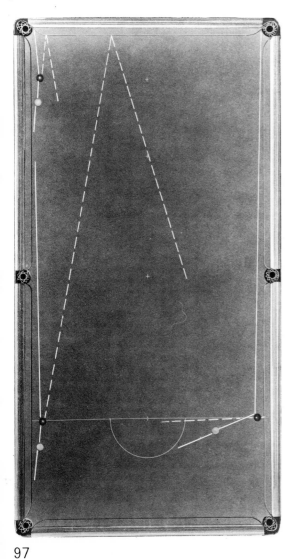

97

98

Shots to Give Pleasure

97. The shot shown on the top left is a run-through red going in-off into the top corner pocket. Use top and lefthand side. This is a little practice shot for the big one to follow! Here the white is played from baulk also with top and lefthand side.

The shot shown on the righthand side is a screw in-off red into the top corner pocket. Use strong righthand side with slightly less than half-ball contact on the red.

98. Pot the red and screw back into the top pocket. Use strong righthand side and keep your head down!

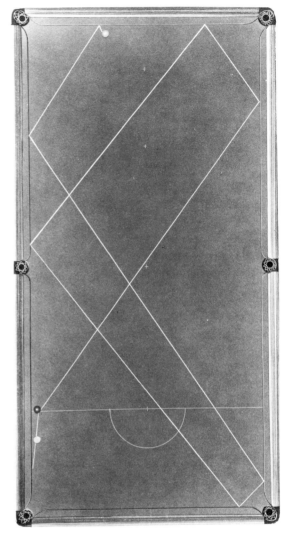

99

100

99. Against the nap. The shot shown on the left is to pot red and bring the cue ball back into the top corner pocket. Strong lefthand side is required with screw.

The shot shown on the right is a long run-through against the nap (the cue ball goes in-off the red into the baulk end corner pocket). Strike the cue ball with top and righthand side.

Learning About Angles (100)

A seven-cushion cannon played with running side with power—a test of good cueing. The lefthand side will take the cue ball round the angles and give free running.

124

The Massé

It is important to create certain tensions throughout the stance for the massé shot. These tensions can be likened to pressures exerted against reasonably strong springs.

First, point the feet in the opposite direction from that in which the cue ball will travel. By placing your feet correctly, you can twist your body into the stroke to create tension on the cue.

Then you turn your left hand to get tension on the tripod of fingers on the cushion rail. The left elbow should be tucked firmly into the side for support.

The cue is pressed very strongly against the thumb of the left hand by leverage exerted from the righthand hold on the butt. Here the right hand thumb pushes hard towards the forefinger, so that if the thumb of the left hand is removed the tip end of the cue will fly up to the ceiling.

It is this tension that holds the cue on a perfectly straight line when you are addressing the ball because you have to get a tremendous amount of spin on the cue ball without too much downward force. It has to be an extremely accurate stroke.

101

102

102 shows a set position for a massé stroke to skirt round the three balls in a row to pot the ball over the middle pocket.

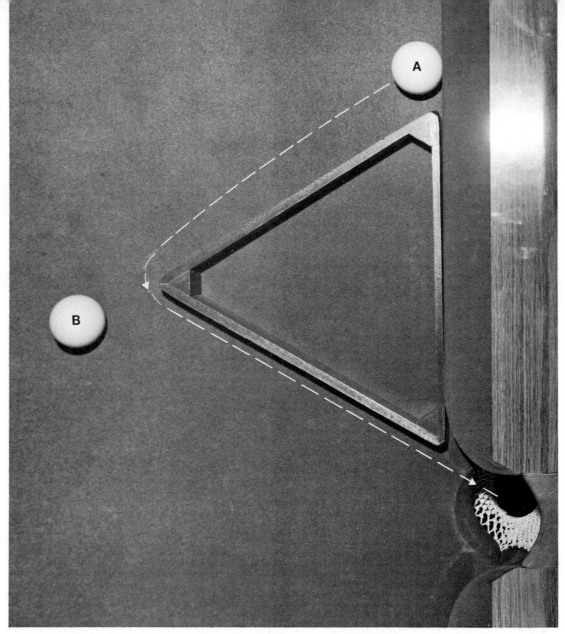

103

In 103 a massé shot on ball A will cause it to take the line indicated. The spin imparted to it will make it hug the side of the triangle without touching ball B until it runs into the centre pocket. Should the cue ball touch the object white on its way it will gain speed and zip down the other side of the triangle.

The massé is a very powerful stroke and should only be played by an expert. I have shown it here to impress you with what is possible on a billiard table, but it is a shot that is very demanding on the cloth and the tip, and unless you have your own table or permission to practise on somebody else's I advise you to leave it alone. It is a beautiful shot to play but purely for fun.